D1143234

£1.50

BAKING

60 SUPER-SPEEDY RECIPES

ON THE TABLE IN... **30** MINUTES

BAKING

60 SUPER-SPEEDY RECIPES

LOVE FOOD™

This edition published by Parragon Books Ltd in 2014
LOVE FOOD is an imprint of Parragon Books Ltd

Parragon Books Ltd
Chartist House
15–17 Trim Street
Bath BA1 1HA, UK
www.parragon.com/lovefood

Copyright © Parragon Books Ltd 2014

LOVE FOOD and the accompanying heart device is a registered trademark of Parragon Books Ltd in Australia, the UK, USA, India and the EU.

All rights reserved. No part of this publication may be reproduced, stored in a retrieval system or transmitted, in any form or by any means, electronic, mechanical, photocopying, recording or otherwise, without the prior permission of the copyright holder.

ISBN 978-1-4723-4440-3

Printed in China

New recipes written by Angela Drake
New photography by Ian Garlick
Designed by Persephone Coelho

Notes for the Reader
This book uses both metric and imperial measurements. Follow the same units of measurement throughout; do not mix metric and imperial. All spoon measurements are level: teaspoons are assumed to be 5 ml, and tablespoons are assumed to be 15 ml. Unless otherwise stated, milk is assumed to be full fat, eggs and individual vegetables are medium, and pepper is freshly ground black pepper. Unless otherwise stated, all root vegetables should be peeled prior to using.

Garnishes, decorations and serving suggestions are all optional and not necessarily included in the recipe ingredients or method. Any optional ingredients and seasoning to taste are not included in the nutritional analysis. The times given are an approximate guide only. Preparation times differ according to the techniques used by different people and the cooking times may also vary from those given. Optional ingredients, variations or serving suggestions have not been included in the time calculations.

CONTENTS

INTRODUCTION

Sometimes there just don't seem to be enough hours in the day to get everything done, and treating family and friends to some home-baked goodies can be the last thing on your mind. But if you can spare just 30 minutes you'll be able to create any one of the gorgeous cakes, cookies, pastries or desserts in this book. With quick cheats and speedy techniques, the use of a few ready-made ingredients and some simple shortcuts, you'll be amazed at what you can achieve in such a short time. It's time to get baking!

The countdown

All the recipes in this book are written with a simple 30-minute countdown. The countdown is divided into three clear and concise steps, each one indicating how many minutes you have left from the start of preparation to the finish of cooking.

Any detailed preparation is included in the steps, along with brief cooling times where necessary. Complete cooling at the end of the recipe is not included in the 30-minute timescale and many of the recipes are served warm from the oven. Use the timings as a basic guide to help you make the recipe, but don't worry if you're a few minutes out either way!

Some recipes include step shots to show the preparation of the dish. As there are three paragraphs in each recipe the step shots are numbered either 1, 2 or 3 to link with them.

Your 30-minute countdown starts here...

Easy! Just four ingredients.

Guide to the tip boxes

Look out for the coloured boxes next to each recipe.

Easy! – ultra simple recipes with a few ingredients that anyone can make. These bakes are a great way to introduce children to baking. Get them to help weigh out ingredients, mix the sponge or dough and shape them.

Time cheat! – when time's at a premium, these tips will help you to save precious minutes.

Freezing! – many of the bakes in this book are perfect for freezing for use another day. Look out for this box and make up a double batch.

Get ahead! – recipes with clever pre-preparation ideas for saving even more time on the day of making.

Just five ingredients! – just a few storecupboard ingredients is all it takes to make these speedy bakes.

All-in-one mix! – save time and energy with these recipes. Simply measure out all the ingredients into one bowl and mix until blended. What could be easier?

Variation! – these tip boxes suggest simple ingredient changes that give you even more variety.

Cook's tip! – helpful hints to ensure success.

9

HINTS AND TIPS FOR QUICK PREP AND COOKING SHORTCUTS

Essential equipment for speedy preparation

Scales and measuring spoons – accurate measuring of ingredients is vital for all baking so a good set of reliable scales is an absolute essential. Digital scales that can be reset as you weigh out each ingredient into one bowl will save valuable time and washing up! A set of graded measuring spoons that fit easily into small tubs and jars will be handy for measuring out small amounts of raising agents, spices or syrups.

Food processor or blender – you'll need one to make light work of time-consuming tasks such as crushing biscuits, making breadcrumbs, puréeing fruit or chopping nuts. Hand-held blenders are also useful for puréeing fruit and making breadcrumbs.

Electric mixer – to whisk light and airy sponges, whip up voluminous meringues or mix buttery cookie dough in just a few minutes you will definitely need a hand-held electric food mixer. Choose one with a powerful motor and variable speed settings for the best results. Although considerably more expensive, a stand-alone mixer with its own stand and large mixing bowl is a great investment. It will save precious time when baking as you are free to get on with other preparation while the mixer is running.

Timer – with all these recipes it's important that baking times are accurate. If you don't have a digital timer on your oven buy a small battery-powered one.

Baking tins and trays – always buy the best quality and sturdiest tins you can afford. Thin, cheap tins may warp or buckle and won't distribute heat well, leading to hot spots and under-cooked patches in cakes and cookies. Non-stick silicone bakeware comes in all shapes and sizes and works especially well for small bakes such as cupcakes and muffins as it doesn't need lining with paper cases. For stability, always place silicone bakeware on a good solid baking sheet before filling and putting in the oven.

Baking paper – lining tins with non-stick baking paper will ensure that all your bakes slide easily out of their tin or tray. To save time, buy packs of pre-cut discs, squares or rectangles. When lining shallow baking trays, allow the paper to hang over the edge of two short sides so you can easily lift out the finished bakes onto a wire rack.

Microwave oven – most modern kitchens have a microwave and it can be an indispensable aid to speedy baking. Use it to melt chocolate, soften butter or warm sauces and syrups. You can even try baking a cake in the microwave (see page 112).

Your 30-minute countdown is getting closer

HINTS AND TIPS FOR QUICK PREP AND COOKING SHORTCUTS

Supermarket cheats and ready-made ingredients

Pastry – ready-made puff, shortcrust and filo pastries are reasonably priced, quick to cook and taste just as good as home-made. To save even more preparation time, buy ready-rolled sheets of pastry that simply need unrolling and cutting to shape before baking.

Canned fruit – keep a selection of canned fruits in the storecupboard for making quick crumbles, tarts and pies in next to no time. Drained canned fruit can also be puréed to make ice-cream sauces or chopped and folded into sponge mixtures.

Ready-to-bake croissant dough – this is perfect for turning into quick sweet pastries with added fillings of butter and sugar, spices, dried fruit or grated chocolate.

Ready-made cake frosting – a little bit sweeter than home-made buttercream but a great storecupboard standby for last-minute cake decoration. Swirl over cakes, pipe on top of cupcakes or use to sandwich together cookies or mini whoopie pies. Chocolate frosting can also be gently warmed for a few seconds in the microwave and used as a quick sauce.

Ready-made sauces – check out supermarket luxury ranges of ready-made fruit, chocolate and toffee sauces. They can transform a simple cake into a special dessert.

Ready-baked pastry cases – available in a variety of sizes from tiny bite-sized tartlets to large flan cases, these are perfect for filling with cream and fruit or quickly baking with sweet fillings. Choose all-butter pastry cases for the best flavour but handle and store carefully as they can be quite fragile.

Top tips for perfect bakes

Make sure you assemble all your ingredients before you start baking. Eggs should be at room temperature and chilled pastry should be removed from the refrigerator about 20 minutes before using.

Most of the recipes in this book require butter to be softened. It's impossible to cream butter with sugar to make cakes and cookie dough unless it has a soft and spreadable consistency. Remove it from the refrigerator at least 30 minutes before baking – longer if the kitchen is cold. To speed up the softening process, unwrap the butter and cut it into cubes. If you forget to remove it before you start, then use a cheese grater to grate the butter coarsely and then spread it out on a warm plate. Alternatively, cut it into small cubes and microwave on the lowest setting in 20-second bursts until soft and pliable.

To chop dried fruit such as apricots, dates or glacé cherries, use a pair of sharp kitchen scissors instead of a knife and chopping board. It's much quicker and you can snip them straight into the mixing bowl.

To speed up the process of melting chocolate, finely chop it with a sharp long-bladed knife before placing in a warmed bowl, or use a coarse cheese grater to grate it into the bowl. If melting in the microwave follow the packet instructions for timings and settings.

Some of the sponge cakes in this book are baked at a higher oven temperature than a traditional sponge recipe. Check cakes a few minutes before the end of the cooking time to make sure that the top is not browning too quickly. If it is, loosely cover the cake with foil for the last few minutes of cooking time.

Most cakes, cookies and small bakes should be left in the baking tin or on the baking sheet for a few minutes to firm up slightly before being transferred to a wire rack to cool.

To speed up the cooling process, remove any lining paper and place the wire rack in a cool, well-ventilated space away from the warm oven. Gently flip over cookies or small bakes after a few minutes.

Chapter 1

QUICK COOKIES

QUICK COOKIES

Cookies really are the ultimate speedy bakes. They are often made with just a few storecupboard ingredients, it's easy to whip up a batch in no time at all and they're baked in a matter of minutes. As far as flavour goes, home-made cookies always beat shop-bought and there's the added satisfaction of knowing exactly what went into them – no baffling chemicals, strange oils and fats, additives or colourings! Whether crisp and crunchy or soft and chewy, a good cookie just can't be beaten, perfect for a home-from-school treat or to serve with a mid-morning cappuccino or an afternoon cup of tea.

In general, home-made cookies are prepared with just a few basic ingredients – butter, sugar, flour and eggs. It makes sense to use the best quality ingredients that you can afford. Butter should be lightly salted or unsalted and, if possible, use free-range eggs. Nuts, chocolate, oats, dried fruits and grated citrus rind are the usual flavourings for cookies and, again, they need to be fresh and of the best quality. It would be a shame to spoil the great flavour of a home-baked cookie with stale nuts, inferior chocolate or out-of-date dried fruit.

Most of the cookies in this chapter are made using the creaming method, where butter and sugar are beaten together until smooth and creamy before adding the other ingredients. The butter needs to be soft and pliable, but not runny, otherwise the dough may spread too much during baking. There's usually no need to chill the dough, but if it's not firm enough to pipe, shape or spoon, then transfer it to a chilled bowl and pop it in the freezer for a few minutes.

Cookies for all occasions!

To ensure that cookies bake evenly it's essential that they are all roughly the same size. If large and small cookies are baked together you'll end up with some that are burnt around the edges and others that are under-cooked. A small ice-cream scoop or measuring spoon can be a quick and efficient way to measure out even-sized amounts. For dough that needs rolling into balls, first shape it into a flat round or long, even-sized roll, then use a knife to cut quickly through the dough to make equal portions.

Most cookie dough can be prepared ahead and kept chilled for 1–2 days, ready for baking at a moment's notice. If you have space in your refrigerator, make up the dough, shape it and transfer to the pre-pared baking sheets. Loosely cover with clingfilm, place in the refrigerator and remove 30 minutes before baking. Firm dough can be placed in polythene bags or freezer bags to save space. Cookie dough freezes well, so make up a double batch. Pack into a freezer box or bag and keep for up to one month. Defrost thoroughly before shaping and baking.

Finally, if any of these delicious cookies are left over at the end of the day you can store them for 2–3 days in an airtight container.

Chocolate Chip Cookies

These American-style, chocolate-laden cookies are crisp on the outside and chewy in the middle. Delicious warm from the oven, they also keep well stored in an airtight container.

Makes 8

INGREDIENTS

unsalted butter, for greasing

125 g/4½ oz margarine

175 g/6 oz plain flour

1 tsp baking powder

85 g/3 oz light muscovado sugar

55 g/2 oz caster sugar

½ tsp vanilla extract

1 egg, beaten

125 g/4½ oz plain chocolate chips

Variation!
Add some roughly chopped nuts to the cookie mixture — try pecan nuts, hazelnuts or blanched almonds.

30 MINS TO GO

Preheat the oven to 190°C/375°F/Gas Mark 5. Lightly grease two baking sheets. Melt the margarine in a small saucepan or in the microwave.

25 MINS TO GO

Place all the ingredients in a large mixing bowl and beat until well combined. Place tablespoons of the mixture on the prepared baking sheets, spaced well apart.

15 MINS TO GO

Bake in the preheated oven for 10–12 minutes, or until golden brown. Leave to cool on the baking sheets for 1–2 minutes, then transfer to a wire rack to cool completely.

Maple Pecan Cookies

These golden nutty cookies are crisp on the outside with a lovely chewy centre. You could replace the nuts with chopped fudge, sultanas or chunks of white or plain chocolate.

Makes 16

INGREDIENTS

70 g/2½ oz pecan nuts

115 g/4 oz butter, softened, plus extra for greasing

100 g/3½ oz dark muscovado sugar

2 tbsp maple syrup

175 g/6 oz self-raising flour

30 MINS TO GO

Preheat the oven to 180°C/350°F/Gas Mark 4. Lightly grease two large baking sheets. Roughly chop the nuts. Put the butter and sugar into a large bowl and beat with a wooden spoon until creamy, then beat in the maple syrup. Sift in the flour and add three quarters of the nuts. Mix to form a rough dough.

20 MINS TO GO

Divide the dough into 16 pieces and roll each piece into a ball. Place the balls on the prepared baking sheets, spaced well apart to allow for spreading. Flatten each ball with your fingers and scatter over the remaining nuts, pressing them lightly into the dough.

15 MINS TO GO

Bake in the preheated oven for 12–14 minutes, or until pale golden. Leave to cool on the baking sheets for 2–3 minutes, then transfer to a wire rack and leave to cool completely.

Cook's tip!
Use a fish slice to transfer the cookies to the wire rack – they will firm up as they cool. For cookies that are crisp throughout, bake for an extra minute.

Snickerdoodles

Popular in America, these crisp and buttery cookies have a lovely cinnamon-sugar coating.

Makes 24

INGREDIENTS

85 g/3 oz butter, softened

175 g/6 oz caster sugar

1 large egg

½ tsp vanilla extract

250 g/9 oz plain flour

1 tsp baking powder

3 tbsp granulated sugar

1 tbsp ground cinnamon

Variation!
Replace 15 g/½ oz of the flour with cocoa powder and add a teaspoonful of instant coffee granules to the cinnamon coating.

30 MINS TO GO

Preheat the oven to 180°C/350°F/Gas Mark 4. Line two large baking sheets with baking paper.

25 MINS TO GO

Put the butter and caster sugar into a bowl and beat together until pale and creamy. Gradually beat in the egg and vanilla extract. Sift together the flour and baking powder and stir into the bowl. Mix to a smooth dough. Divide the dough into 24 pieces and shape each piece into a ball.

20 MINS TO GO

Mix together the granulated sugar and cinnamon on a plate. Roll the balls in the mixture. Place on the prepared baking sheets, spaced well apart. Flatten slightly with your fingers. Bake in the preheated oven for 12–14 minutes, or until golden. Leave to cool on the baking sheets for 5 minutes, then transfer to a wire rack to cool completely.

Butter Cookies

These dainty, melt-in-the-mouth cookies are made with just a few simple ingredients. They will keep in an airtight container for up to five days.

Makes 24

INGREDIENTS

175 g/6 oz lightly salted butter, softened, plus extra for greasing

50 g/1¾ oz icing sugar

200 g/7 oz plain flour

½ tsp baking powder

12 glacé cherries, halved

30 MINS TO GO

Preheat the oven to 190°C/375°F/Gas Mark 5. Lightly grease two large baking sheets. Place the butter in a large bowl and beat with a hand-held electric mixer until very soft and pale. Sift in the icing sugar, flour and baking powder and stir to combine. Beat with the mixer for 1–2 minutes to make a creamy paste.

20 MINS TO GO

Spoon the mixture into a piping bag fitted with a 1-cm/½-inch fluted nozzle. Pipe 24 rosettes onto the prepared baking sheets. Place half a glacé cherry in the centre of each rosette.

15 MINS TO GO

Bake in the preheated oven for 9–11 minutes, or until just set and pale golden around the edges. Leave to cool on the baking sheets for 3–4 minutes, then transfer to a wire rack and leave to cool completely.

Time cheat!
If you don't want to pipe the cookie mixture, use 2 teaspoons to drop walnut-sized blobs of the paste onto the baking sheets. Flatten them slightly with a spoon.

24

Coconut & Cranberry Cookies

Sweet desiccated coconut perfectly complements the sharpness of the dried cranberries in these crumbly cookies.

Makes 20

INGREDIENTS

225 g/8 oz butter, softened
140 g/5 oz caster sugar
1 egg yolk
2 tsp vanilla extract
280 g/10 oz plain flour
pinch of salt
40 g/1½ oz desiccated coconut
60 g/2¼ oz dried cranberries

30 MINS TO GO

Preheat the oven to 190°C/375°F/Gas Mark 5. Line two baking sheets with baking paper.

25 MINS TO GO

Put the butter and sugar into a bowl and beat together until pale and creamy, then beat in the egg yolk and vanilla extract. Sift together the flour and salt into the mixture, add the coconut and cranberries and stir until thoroughly combined.

20 MINS TO GO

Place tablespoons of the mixture on the prepared baking sheets, spaced well apart. Bake in the preheated oven for 12–15 minutes, or until golden brown. Leave to cool on the baking sheets for 1–2 minutes, then transfer to wire racks to cool.

Freezing!
Freeze the baked cookies for up to one month. Thaw at room temperature for 1–2 hours.

Easy! Just four ingredients.

Makes 16–18

INGREDIENTS

85 g/3 oz unsalted butter, plus extra for greasing

175 g/6 oz chocolate hazelnut spread

70 g/2½ oz blanched hazelnuts

175 g/6 oz rolled oats

Chocolate, Nut & Oat Cookies

These deliciously nutty treats are simplicity itself to prepare.

30 MINS TO GO

Preheat the oven to 200°C/400°F/Gas Mark 6. Grease a large baking sheet.

25 MINS TO GO

Place the butter and chocolate hazelnut spread in a saucepan and heat gently until just melted. Chop the hazelnuts coarsely. Add the oats and chopped hazelnuts to the chocolate mixture and stir to combine thoroughly.

20 MINS TO GO

Shape the mixture into 16–18 equal-sized balls, then press onto the prepared baking sheet. Bake in the preheated oven for 10–12 minutes. Remove from the oven and leave until firm before transferring to a wire rack to cool.

Shortbread

Just a few simple ingredients combine to make this melt-in-the-mouth classic Scottish bake. Choose the finest quality ingredients for the best flavour.

Makes 8

INGREDIENTS

125 g/4½ oz lightly salted butter, softened, plus extra for greasing

55 g/2 oz caster sugar, plus extra for sprinkling

150 g/5½ oz plain flour

25 g/1 oz cornflour

Variation!
Cornflour gives shortbread a lovely soft and crumbly texture. If you prefer your shortbread a little crunchier, replace the cornflour with ground rice and bake for an extra 2–3 minutes.

30 MINS TO GO

Preheat the oven to 190°C/375°F/Gas Mark 5. Lightly grease a baking sheet and a 20-cm/8-inch metal flan ring. Place the ring on the prepared baking sheet. Put the butter and sugar into a large bowl and beat with a wooden spoon until very creamy. Sift in the flour and cornflour and mix until crumbly.

25 MINS TO GO

Gather the mixture together with your hands and knead gently to form a smooth dough. Press the dough into the ring and, using your knuckles, spread to the edge. Level the surface with a small angled palette knife. Prick the dough all over with a fork and mark into 8 triangles with a knife.

20 MINS TO GO

Bake in the preheated oven for 15–20 minutes, or until golden around the edge. Carefully cut the hot shortbread into the triangles and sprinkle liberally with sugar. Gently remove the ring and leave the shortbread to cool on the baking sheet.

Dried Fruit & Sunflower Seed Cookies

These soft, chewy cookies are full of juicy sultanas and crunchy sunflower seeds.

Makes 18

INGREDIENTS

85 g/3 oz unsalted butter, softened, plus extra for greasing

85 g/3 oz light muscovado sugar

1 egg

225 g/8 oz plain flour

½ tsp grated nutmeg

55 g/2 oz sultanas

30 g/1 oz sunflower seeds

demerara sugar, for sprinkling

30 MINS TO GO

Preheat the oven to 200°C/400°F/Gas Mark 6. Lightly grease a large baking sheet.

25 MINS TO GO

Put the butter and muscovado sugar into a mixing bowl and beat together until soft and fluffy. Add the egg and beat thoroughly, then stir in the flour, nutmeg, sultanas and sunflower seeds, mixing evenly to a fairly soft dough.

20 MINS TO GO

Break off small pieces of the dough and use your hands to roll them into walnut-sized balls. Arrange the balls on the prepared baking sheet and press to flatten slightly. Sprinkle the cookies with a little demerara sugar and bake in the preheated oven for 12–15 minutes, or until golden brown. Transfer to a wire rack to cool.

Easy!
Children will love helping to make these nutty treats.

Peanut Butter Biscuits

These biscuits are bursting with peanut flavour and have a lovely oaty texture.

Makes 26

INGREDIENTS

115 g/4 oz butter, softened

125 g/4½ oz crunchy peanut butter

100 g/3½ oz caster sugar

115 g/4 oz soft light brown sugar

1 egg

½ tsp vanilla extract

85 g/3 oz plain flour

½ tsp bicarbonate of soda

½ tsp baking powder

pinch of salt

140 g/5 oz rolled oats

30 MINS TO GO

Preheat the oven to 180°C/350°F/Gas Mark 4. Line several baking sheets with baking paper.

25 MINS TO GO

Place the butter and peanut butter in a bowl and beat together. Beat in the caster sugar and brown sugar, then gradually beat in the egg and vanilla extract. Sift together the flour, bicarbonate of soda, baking powder and salt into the bowl, then stir in the oats.

15 MINS TO GO

Place spoonfuls of the mixture on the baking sheets, spaced well apart to allow for spreading. Flatten slightly with a fork. Bake in the preheated oven for 12 minutes or until lightly browned. Leave to cool on the sheets for 2 minutes, then transfer to wire racks to cool completely.

S'mores

An American and Canadian treat traditionally cooked over a campfire. Buttery cookies are sandwiched with marshmallows and topped with melting chocolate.

Makes 18

INGREDIENTS

sunflower oil, for oiling

175 g/6 oz wholemeal flour, plus extra for dusting

2 tsp baking powder

55 g/2 oz rolled oats

55 g/2 oz caster sugar

150 g/5½ oz unsalted butter, chilled

2 egg yolks

200 g/7 oz plain chocolate

18 marshmallows

Time cheat!
Use ready-made digestive biscuits and pop into a preheated oven at 180°C/350°F/Gas Mark 4 for 4–6 minutes to melt the chocolate and marshmallows.

30 MINS TO GO

Preheat the oven to 180°C/350°F/Gas Mark 4. Lightly oil two baking sheets. Mix the flour, baking powder, oats and sugar together in a bowl. Cut the butter into pieces and rub it in until the mixture resembles fine breadcrumbs. Stir in the egg yolks and press the dough together to make a ball.

20 MINS TO GO

Knead the dough on a lightly floured work surface, then roll it out thinly. Stamp out 6-cm/2½-inch rounds and transfer to the prepared sheets. Reroll the trimmings until you have 36 rounds. Bake in the preheated oven for 12–15 minutes, or until golden brown.

5 MINS TO GO

Break the chocolate into 18 pieces and add a piece to 18 hot biscuits and a marshmallow to the remaining 18 biscuits. Leave to stand for 1–2 minutes, then sandwich the biscuits together in pairs with the marshmallows in the centre and the chocolate on top. Serve warm or cold.

Apple & Oatmeal Cookies

Chunks of sweet apple, oats and raisins combine to make these deliciously moist and crumbly cookies.

Makes 26

INGREDIENTS

1 large apple

1 tsp lemon juice

225 g/8 oz butter, softened, plus extra for greasing

100 g/3½ oz soft light brown sugar

100 g/3½ oz caster sugar

1 egg

225 g/8 oz self-raising flour

150 g/5½ oz rolled oats

85 g/3 oz raisins

Variation!
Add some roughly chopped nuts to the cookie mixture – try pecan nuts, hazelnuts or blanched almonds.

30 MINS TO GO

Preheat the oven to 180°C/350°F/Gas Mark 4. Grease three large baking sheets. Peel, core and finely dice the apple and toss it in the lemon juice.

25 MINS TO GO

Place the butter, brown sugar and caster sugar in a bowl and beat together until creamy. Gradually beat in the egg. Sift in the flour and add the oats, raisins and apple. Mix until thoroughly combined. Place dessertspoons of the mixture on the prepared baking sheets, spaced well apart.

20 MINS TO GO

Bake in the preheated oven for 12–15 minutes, or until golden around the edges. Leave to cool on the baking sheets for 5–10 minutes, or until firm enough to transfer to a wire rack to cool completely.

Lemon Fork Cookies

If you fancy some crisp, buttery cookies with your morning cuppa, this recipe can't be beaten. They taste divine warm from the oven— you may need to make a double batch!

Makes 16

INGREDIENTS

115 g/4 oz unsalted butter, softened, plus extra for greasing

55 g/2 oz caster sugar

finely grated rind of 1 small lemon

175 g/6 oz self-raising flour

Variation!
Replace the lemon rind with orange rind or with 1 tsp vanilla extract or coffee extract. To make chocolate fork cookies replace 2 tbsp of the flour with cocoa powder.

30 MINS TO GO

Preheat the oven to 180°C/350°F/Gas Mark 4. Lightly grease two large baking sheets. Put the butter into a large bowl and beat with a wooden spoon for 1 minute until very soft. Gradually beat in the sugar and lemon rind.

25 MINS TO GO

Sift in the flour and mix until crumbly. Gather together with your hands and knead lightly to form a dough. Divide the dough into 16 pieces and shape each piece into a walnut-sized ball. Place the balls on the prepared baking sheets, spaced well apart to allow for spreading. Dip the prongs of a fork into cold water, then use to flatten each ball of dough.

20 MINS TO GO

Bake in the preheated oven for 12–15 minutes, or until pale golden. Leave to cool on the baking sheets for 1–2 minutes, then transfer to a wire rack to cool completely.

White Chocolate & Macadamia Nut Cookies

These cookies are generously dotted with delicious chunks of white chocolate and rich macadamia nuts.

Makes 16

INGREDIENTS

115 g/4 oz butter, softened, plus extra for greasing

115 g/4 oz soft light brown sugar

1 tbsp golden syrup

175 g/6 oz self-raising flour

55 g/2 oz macadamia nuts

55 g/2 oz white chocolate

Cook's tip!
If the cookies have spread during baking, reshape them with a knife when they come out of the oven.

30 MINS TO GO

Preheat the oven to 180°C/350°F/Gas Mark 4. Grease two large baking sheets.

25 MINS TO GO

Put the butter and sugar into a bowl and beat together until pale and creamy, then beat in the golden syrup. Sift in the flour, add the roughly chopped nuts and mix to form a rough dough. Divide the dough into 16 even-sized balls and place on the prepared baking sheet, spaced well apart. Slightly flatten each ball with your fingertips.

15 MINS TO GO

Chop the chocolate into chunks and top the balls with these, pressing them lightly into the dough. Bake in the preheated oven for 12–14 minutes, or until just set and pale golden. Leave to cool on the baking sheets for 1–2 minutes, then transfer to a wire rack to cool completely.

Birthday Cookie Surprises

Jazz up ready-made biscuits with icing, piping and lots of colourful sugar sprinkles and no one will ever know that you cheated!

Makes 12

INGREDIENTS

175 g/6 oz icing sugar

5–6 tsp lukewarm water

pink and yellow food colouring paste

12 ready-made cookies (such as digestives, rich tea or butter thins)

2 tbsp multi-coloured non-pareils

2 tsp polka dot or confetti sprinkles

Variation!
For Christmas cookies, colour the icing red and green and decorate with star-shaped sprinkles, or pipe simple snowflake designs in white icing.

30 MINS TO GO

Sift the icing sugar into a bowl and gradually beat in the water to make a smooth, thick icing. Divide the icing between four bowls. Leave 1 bowl white, then use the colouring pastes to colour 1 bowl pale pink, 1 bowl deep pink and 1 bowl pale yellow.

20 MINS TO GO

Spread the white icing over 4 cookies, then liberally sprinkle the tops with the non-pareils to cover the icing completely. Transfer to a wire rack to set. Top 4 cookies with the yellow icing and scatter over the sprinkles. Transfer to the wire rack to set.

10 MINS TO GO

Spread the remaining 4 cookies with the pale pink icing and transfer to the wire rack. Spoon the deep pink icing into a piping bag fitted with a fine writing nozzle and pipe initials, numbers or patterns on the iced cookies. Leave to set on the wire rack.

Easy!
Just four
ingredients.

Makes 12

INGREDIENTS

**175 g/6 oz plain flour,
plus extra for dusting**

175 g/6 oz butter, chilled

**200 g/7 oz caster sugar,
plus extra for dusting**

1 tsp vanilla extract

Vanilla Sugar Biscuits

These delicately flavoured heart-shaped biscuits would be perfect as a Valentine's Day gift.

30 MINS TO GO

Preheat the oven to 180°C/350°F/Gas Mark 4. Line two baking sheets with baking paper.

25 MINS TO GO

Sift the flour into a large bowl. Cut the butter into pieces and rub it in until the mixture resembles fine breadcrumbs. Stir in the sugar and vanilla extract and mix to a firm dough.

20 MINS TO GO

Roll out the dough on a lightly floured work surface to a thickness of 1 cm/½ inch. Stamp out 12 biscuits with a heart-shaped cutter and arrange on the prepared sheets. Bake in the preheated oven for about 15 minutes until just coloured. Transfer to a wire rack and leave to cool completely. Dust with sugar just before serving.

Chapter 2

SPEEDY SMALL BAKES

SPEEDY SMALL BAKES

When only something sweet will hit the spot be it a cupcake, muffin or mini whoopie pie then you need to look no further than this chapter. It's full of bite-sized goodies that are super speedy to make and taste fantastic too. All these small bakes are perfect for feeding a crowd in a hurry and as well as the usual favourites we've included quick cake pops, baked doughnuts, fruity French friands and some sensational mini pecan pies!

The beauty of making individual cakes when you're short on time is the relatively quick baking time - just 15-20 minutes in a hot oven is all it takes to produce a tempting tray of muffins or cupcakes. With no time for icing or decoration it's all down to adding flavourings to the basic recipe in the form of chocolate, fruit or spices to give added appeal. Once you've tried a few recipes in this chapter

you'll see how easy it is to substitute or experiment with flavour variations. For example, replace chocolate chips with fudge pieces, swap lemon for orange or lime or add chopped nuts for extra bite.

Many of the bakes in this chapter are ideal for children's parties, especially the cupcakes and cake pops. The recipes are easy to double up and also freeze well. Cool cupcakes completely before packing into freezer-proof boxes interleaved with baking paper. Remove from the freezer 3-4 hours before serving to allow them to defrost thoroughly. Cake pops can be made 2-3 days in advance and stored in the refrigerator. To give as party favours, wrap each cake pop in cellophane and tie with ribbon and a label with each child's name on it.

Scones make the perfect teatime treat and always taste best served on the day

Tasty treats in no time!

day of making. Remember you need a light touch when handling the dough as over-kneading will result in a heavy, dense texture and don't be tempted to roll the dough too thinly. For breakfast, brunch or a mid-morning snack, warm muffins straight from the oven or lightly spiced doughnuts are just the ticket. When making muffins take care not to over-mix – the batter should be slightly lumpy. Make sure the oven is preheated to the correct temperature to achieve a good quick rise.

For a classic afternoon tea why not serve a selection of these quick bakes? As they're all so quick to make, just a couple of hours spent in the kitchen will result in a wonderful spread of delectable goodies. Allow 2-3 cakes per person and serve on pretty cake stands or arrange in neat rows on large serving platters.

And of course all of these delightful mini marvels make great desserts too. A dollop of cream or hot custard spooned over a warm cupcake is the ideal winter warming pudding whilst a hot muffin served with a scoop of ice cream and a drizzle of chocolate sauce is the perfect finale for any family dinner!

55

Makes 12

INGREDIENTS

100 g/3½ oz self-raising flour

100 g/3½ oz butter, softened

100 g/3½ oz caster sugar

2 large eggs

100 g/3½ oz plain chocolate chips

Chocolate Chip Cupcakes

For a change, you could use a mixture of milk chocolate or white chocolate chips or add a swirl of ready-made chocolate frosting.

30 MINS TO GO

Preheat the oven to 190°C/375°F/Gas Mark 5. Line a 12-hole bun tin with paper cases.

25 MINS TO GO

Sift the flour into a large bowl. Add the butter, sugar and eggs and beat until smooth. Fold in the chocolate chips. Spoon the mixture into the paper cases.

20 MINS TO GO

Bake in the preheated oven for 20 minutes, or until risen, golden and firm to the touch. Transfer to a wire rack and leave to cool completely.

Mini Chocolate Whoopie Pies

Who would have thought you could make these divine bite-sized chocolate treats in such a short time? For a special occasion replace the chocolate spread with whipped cream and jam.

Makes 22

INGREDIENTS

100 g/3½ oz butter, softened

125 g/4½ oz dark muscovado sugar

1 egg, lightly beaten

½ tsp vanilla extract

175 g/6 oz self-raising flour

25 g/1 oz cocoa powder

5 tbsp milk

4–5 tbsp chocolate and hazelnut spread

30 MINS TO GO

Preheat the oven to 190°C/375°F/Gas Mark 5. Line two large baking sheets with baking paper. Put the butter and sugar into a large bowl and beat with a hand-held electric mixer for 1–2 minutes. Whisk in the egg and vanilla extract. Sift in the flour and cocoa powder, add the milk and fold in gently until thoroughly combined.

25 MINS TO GO

Pipe or spoon 44 small mounds of the mixture onto the prepared baking sheet. Each mound should be about 4 cm/1½ inches in diameter. Bake in the preheated oven for 7–8 minutes, or until just firm. Carefully transfer the hot cakes to a wire rack using a palette knife. Leave to cool for 10 minutes.

5 MINS TO GO

Sandwich the cakes together with the chocolate and hazelnut spread. If the spread starts to soften because the cakes are still slightly warm, pop the filled whoopie pies in the refrigerator for a few minutes until completely cold.

Cook's tip!
To speed up the cooling process, gently flip the cakes over on the wire rack after 5 minutes.

58

Blueberry Scones

These soft scone wedges are bursting with fresh blueberries and are delicious split and lightly buttered warm from the oven.

Makes 8

INGREDIENTS

250 g/9 oz plain flour, plus extra for dusting

2 tsp baking powder

¼ tsp salt

85 g/3 oz butter, chilled, plus extra for greasing and to serve

70 g/2½ oz golden caster sugar

115 g/4 oz blueberries

1 egg

100 ml/3½ fl oz buttermilk

1 tbsp milk

1 tbsp demerara sugar

Cook's tip!
Use frozen blueberries if you can't get fresh – stir them in to the mixture while still frozen to avoid colour bleed.

30 MINS TO GO

Preheat the oven to 200°C/400°F/Gas Mark 6. Lightly grease a large baking sheet.

25 MINS TO GO

Sift together the flour, baking powder and salt into a bowl. Cut the butter into pieces and rub in until the mixture resembles fine breadcrumbs. Stir in the caster sugar and blueberries. Beat together the egg and buttermilk and pour into the bowl. Mix to a soft dough. Turn out onto a floured work surface, knead gently, then shape into an 18-cm/7-inch round.

20 MINS TO GO

Cut the round into 8 wedges and transfer to the prepared baking sheet. Brush the tops with milk and sprinkle with demerara sugar. Bake in the preheated oven for 18–20 minutes, or until risen and golden brown. Transfer to a wire rack to cool, then serve with butter.

Rocky Road Chocolate Muffins

These tempting chocolate muffins are made even more delicious with the addition of white chocolate and gooey marshmallow.

Makes 12

INGREDIENTS

225 g/8 oz plain flour

55 g/2 oz cocoa powder

1 tbsp baking powder

pinch of salt

50 g/1¾ oz white mini marshmallows

115 g/4 oz caster sugar

100 g/3½ oz white chocolate chips

85 g/3 oz butter

2 eggs

250 ml/9 fl oz milk

30 MINS TO GO

Preheat the oven to 200°C/400°F/Gas Mark 6. Line a 12-hole muffin tin with paper cases. Sift together the flour, cocoa powder, baking powder and salt into a large bowl. Cut the marshmallows in half and stir in with the sugar and chocolate chips. Melt the butter and leave to cool.

25 MINS TO GO

Lightly beat the eggs in a large bowl, then beat in the milk and butter. Make a well in the centre of the dry ingredients and pour in the beaten liquid ingredients. Gently stir until just combined; do not over-mix.

20 MINS TO GO

Spoon the mixture into the paper cases. Bake in the preheated oven for 18–20 minutes, or until risen and firm to the touch. Leave to cool in the tin for 1–2 minutes, then serve warm or transfer to a wire rack and leave to cool completely.

Cake Pops

Kids will love helping to make these speedy sweet treats, although it may get a bit messy! Don't worry if the coating looks a little uneven – just disguise it with plenty of sugar sprinkles.

Makes 8

INGREDIENTS

175 g/6 oz ready-made sponge cake (chocolate or vanilla flavour)

70 g/2½ oz ready-made chocolate fudge frosting, at room temperature

175 g/6 oz yellow or pink candy melts

star- and polka-dot-shaped sugar sprinkles, to decorate

you will also need 8 cake pop sticks

30 MINS TO GO

Crumble the sponge cake into a bowl. Add the frosting and beat with a wooden spoon until thoroughly mixed. Use your hands to divide and shape the mixture into 8 firm, walnut-sized balls.

25 MINS TO GO

Place the balls on a plate and put in the freezer for 10–12 minutes. Meanwhile, place the candy melts in a heatproof bowl set over a saucepan of gently simmering water and heat until just melted. Remove from the heat and stir until smooth. Leave to cool for 5 minutes.

10 MINS TO GO

Remove the cake balls from the freezer. Dip the end of a cake pop stick in the melted candy and push into the centre of a cake ball. Using a small palette knife cover the cake ball with melted candy, then sprinkle liberally with sugar sprinkles. Stand in a tall glass (see Tip) and place in the refrigerator for a few minutes to set. Repeat with the remaining cake balls, melted candy and sprinkles.

Cook's tip!
Fill the tall glass with dried beans or rice to stop the weight of the cake pops from tipping the glass over.

Molten Chocolate Cupcakes

These indulgent cupcakes have a luxurious melted chocolate centre.

Makes 9

INGREDIENTS

175 g/6 oz soft margarine
175 g/6 oz caster sugar
3 large eggs
250 g/9 oz self-raising flour
3 tbsp cocoa powder
9 squares plain chocolate
icing sugar, for dusting

30 MINS TO GO

Preheat the oven to 190°C/375°F/Gas Mark 5. Line a 9-hole bun tin with paper cases.

25 MINS TO GO

Put the margarine, caster sugar, eggs, flour and cocoa powder in a large bowl and beat together until just smooth. Spoon half of the mixture into the paper cases. Using a teaspoon, make an indentation in the centre of each cake. Place a square of chocolate in each indentation, then spoon the remaining cake mixture on top.

20 MINS TO GO

Bake the cupcakes in the preheated oven for 18–20 minutes, or until well risen and springy to the touch. Leave to cool for 2–3 minutes before serving warm, dusted with icing sugar.

Variation!
These make a delicious
dessert served with whipped
cream or a scoop of vanilla
ice cream.

Cinnamon Buns

Making cinnamon buns from scratch can be time-consuming, but this cheat's version using a can of croissant dough looks and tastes just as good.

Makes 8

INGREDIENTS

40 g/1½ oz light muscovado sugar

40 g/1½ oz butter, softened, plus extra for greasing

1½ tsp ground cinnamon

250 g/9 oz ready-to-bake canned croissants

40 g/1½ oz icing sugar, sifted

1½ tsp lukewarm water

30 MINS TO GO

Preheat the oven to 200°C/400°F/Gas Mark 6. Lightly grease 8 holes of a 12-hole muffin tin. Put the sugar into a bowl with the butter and cinnamon and beat until smooth.

25 MINS TO GO

Unroll the croissant dough but don't separate it into triangles. Spread the cinnamon butter along the length of the croissant dough. Gently roll up the dough from one short side. Using a sharp knife, slice the roll into 8 rounds. Place 1 round, flat-side down, in each of the 8 holes in the prepared tin, pressing down gently.

20 MINS TO GO

Bake in the preheated oven for 10–14 minutes until risen and golden. Meanwhile, mix the sugar and water in a small bowl to make a smooth icing. Leave the buns to cool in the tin for 1–2 minutes, then transfer to a wire rack. Using a teaspoon, drizzle the icing over the hot buns. Serve warm or cold.

Cook's tip!
Take care not to stretch the dough when unrolling it or the perforations may tear. If this happens, just overlap the edges and press down firmly to re-join.

Blueberry Muffins

Dotted with juicy blueberries and flavoured with lemon and vanilla, these buttery muffins will be snapped up as soon as they come out of the oven.

Makes 12

INGREDIENTS

280 g/10 oz plain flour

1 tbsp baking powder

pinch of salt

115 g/4 oz soft light brown sugar

150 g/5½ oz frozen blueberries

85 g/3 oz butter

2 eggs

250 ml/9 fl oz milk

1 tsp vanilla extract

grated rind of 1 lemon

30 MINS TO GO

Preheat the oven to 200°C/400°F/Gas Mark 6. Line a 12-hole muffin tin with paper cases. Sift together the flour, baking powder and salt into a large bowl. Stir in the sugar and blueberries. Melt the butter and leave to cool slightly.

25 MINS TO GO

Lightly beat the eggs in a large jug, then beat in the milk, butter, vanilla extract and lemon rind. Make a well in the centre of the dry ingredients and pour in the beaten liquid ingredients. Stir gently until just combined; do not over-mix.

20 MINS TO GO

Divide the mixture between the paper cases. Bake in the preheated oven for 18–20 minutes until well-risen, golden brown and firm to the touch. Leave to cool in the tin for 1–2 minutes, then serve warm or transfer to a wire rack and leave to cool completely.

Freezing!
Baked muffins can be frozen for up to 6 months once they are completely cool. Wrap well in polythene bags or airtight containers and defrost at room temperature for 2-3 hours.

White Chocolate & Raspberry Muffins

Best eaten warm from the oven, these muffins make a great mid-morning snack.

Makes 12

INGREDIENTS

250 g/9 oz plain flour

1 tbsp baking powder

115 g/4 oz caster sugar

85 g/3 oz butter, chilled

1 large egg

175 ml/6 fl oz milk

175 g/6 oz raspberries

140 g/5 oz white chocolate chips

30 MINS TO GO

Preheat the oven to 200°C/400°F/Gas Mark 6. Line a 12-hole muffin tin with paper cases. Sift together the flour and baking powder into a large bowl and stir in the sugar. Grate the butter roughly and stir in with a fork to coat in the flour mixture.

25 MINS TO GO

Lightly beat the egg in a jug, then beat in the milk. Make a well in the centre of the dry ingredients and pour in the liquid ingredients. Stir gently until just combined; do not over-mix. Fold in the raspberries and half the chocolate chips.

20 MINS TO GO

Divide the mixture between the paper cases and scatter over the remaining chocolate chips. Bake in the preheated oven for 18–20 minutes, or until risen, golden and just firm to the touch. Leave to cool for 1–2 minutes, then transfer to a wire rack to cool completely.

Variation!
Replace the raspberries with fresh or frozen blackberries, or try chopped fresh mango for a tropical flavour.

Sugar & Spice Doughnuts

Try this easy baked version for a quick doughnut fix. Best served warm from the oven, they will keep in an airtight container for a couple of days.

Makes 6 or 12

INGREDIENTS

115 g/4 oz self-raising flour

½ tsp baking powder

70 g/2½ oz caster sugar

1 tsp ground mixed spice

75 ml/2½ fl oz milk

1 egg, beaten

½ tsp vanilla extract

25 g/1 oz butter, melted, plus extra for greasing

sugar coating

2 tbsp caster sugar

1 tsp ground mixed spice

Cook's tip!
If you don't have a doughnut tin, divide the mixture between the holes of a 12-hole mini muffin tin and bake for 10–12 minutes. They'll taste just as good!

30 MINS TO GO

Preheat the oven to 190°C/375°F/Gas Mark 5. Thoroughly grease a 6-hole doughnut tin or a 12-hole mini muffin tin. Sift together the flour and baking powder into a bowl and stir in the sugar and spice. Make a well in the centre. Mix together the milk, egg, vanilla extract and melted butter and pour into the well. Mix with a wooden spoon until smooth.

25 MINS TO GO

Spoon the mixture into a piping bag fitted with a plain nozzle (twist the bag around the nozzle before filling to prevent the mixture leaking out, then untwist when ready to pipe). Pipe the mixture as neatly as possible into the prepared tin. Each hole should be about two-thirds full.

20 MINS TO GO

Bake in the preheated oven for 12–14 minutes, or until risen, golden and firm to the touch. To make the sugar coating, mix together the sugar and mixed spice on a plate. Leave the doughnuts to cool in the tin for 2–3 minutes, then gently ease them out. Toss them in the spiced sugar to coat completely and serve warm or cold.

Chocolate & Cream Cheese Cupcakes

The combination of cream cheese and chocolate gives these delicious cupcakes an indulgently gooey texture.

Makes 12

INGREDIENTS

175 g/6 oz plain flour

20 g/¾ oz cocoa powder

¾ tsp bicarbonate of soda

200 g/7 oz caster sugar

50 ml/2 fl oz sunflower oil

175 ml/6 fl oz water

2 tsp white vinegar

½ tsp vanilla extract

150 g/5½ oz full-fat cream cheese

1 egg

100 g/3½ oz plain chocolate chips

30 MINS TO GO

Preheat the oven to 180°C/350°F/Gas Mark 4. Line a 12-hole muffin tin with paper cases. Sift together the flour, cocoa powder and bicarbonate of soda into a large bowl. Stir 150 g/5½ oz of the sugar into the flour mixture. Add the oil, water, vinegar and vanilla extract and stir to combine.

25 MINS TO GO

Place the remaining sugar, the cream cheese and egg in a large bowl and beat well. Stir in the chocolate chips.

20 MINS TO GO

Spoon the cake mixture into the paper cases and top with a spoonful of the cream cheese mixture. Bake in the preheated oven for 18–20 minutes, or until risen and firm to the touch. Transfer to a wire rack and leave to cool.

Fudge Nut Muffins

Peanut butter and vanilla fudge give these rich muffins wonderful flavour and texture.

Makes 12

INGREDIENTS

250 g/9 oz plain flour

4 tsp baking powder

85 g/3 oz caster sugar

6 tbsp crunchy peanut butter

55 g/2 oz butter

1 large egg

175 ml/6 fl oz milk

150 g/5½ oz vanilla fudge

3 tbsp unsalted peanuts

30 MINS TO GO

Preheat the oven to 200°C/400°F/Gas Mark 6. Line a 12-hole muffin tin with paper cases. Sift together the flour and baking powder into a small bowl. Stir in the sugar. Add the peanut butter and stir until the mixture resembles breadcrumbs. Transfer to a large bowl. Melt the butter and leave to cool.

25 MINS TO GO

Lightly beat the egg in a large jug, then beat in the milk and butter. Make a well in the centre of the dry ingredients, pour in the liquid ingredients. Cut the fudge into small pieces and add. Stir gently until just combined; do not over-mix.

20 MINS TO GO

Divide the mixture between the paper cases. Chop the peanuts roughly and sprinkle on top of the muffins. Bake in the preheated oven for 18–20 minutes, or until well risen, golden brown and firm to the touch. Leave to cool in the tin for 1–2 minutes, then serve warm or transfer to a wire rack and leave to cool completely.

Cook's tip!
To refresh day-old muffins, place them on a baking tray and heat in the oven for 5–10 minutes at 180°C/350°F/Gas Mark 4.

Blueberry & Lemon Friands

These soft little French cakes have a sweet almond flavour. To achieve the classic oval shape you'll need a friand mould, but you can use a muffin tin instead.

Makes 8

INGREDIENTS

115 g/4 oz unsalted butter, diced, plus extra for greasing

3 large egg whites

pinch of salt

55 g/2 oz plain flour

150 g/5½ oz icing sugar, plus extra for dusting

85 g/3 oz ground almonds

1 tsp finely grated lemon rind

55 g/2 oz blueberries

Time cheat!
To save time, melt the butter in the microwave oven. Heat on medium–low in 10-second bursts until the butter is just runny.

30 MINS TO GO

Preheat the oven to 220°C/425°F/Gas Mark 7. Put the butter into a saucepan and melt over a low heat. Pour into a shallow bowl and leave to cool for a few minutes. Thoroughly grease an 8-hole silicone friand mould or 8 holes of a non-stick muffin tin, then place on a baking sheet.

25 MINS TO GO

Put the egg whites and salt into a large, grease-free bowl and beat with a hand-held electric mixer for 1–2 minutes until foaming and floppy, but not stiff. Sift in the flour and icing sugar and fold into the egg whites with the ground almonds and lemon rind. Fold in the melted butter to make a smooth batter.

20 MINS TO GO

Spoon the batter evenly into the prepared mould and scatter over the blueberries. Bake in the preheated oven for 14–18 minutes until risen, golden and just firm to the touch. Leave to cool in the mould for 5 minutes, then turn out onto a wire rack to cool completely. Serve warm or cold dusted with icing sugar.

Apple Streusel Cupcakes

Spiced apple combines with a crunchy topping in these stunning cupcakes — serve them warm with whipped cream for a delicious impromptu dessert.

Makes 14

INGREDIENTS

½ tsp bicarbonate of soda

280 g/10 oz apple sauce

55 g/2 oz butter, softened

85 g/3 oz demerara sugar

1 large egg

175 g/6 oz self-raising flour

½ tsp ground cinnamon

½ tsp grated nutmeg

topping

50 g/1¾ oz plain flour

50 g/1¾ oz demerara sugar

ground cinnamon or grated
   nutmeg, to taste

35 g/1¼ oz butter, diced

30 MINS TO GO

Preheat the oven to 180°C/350°F/Gas Mark 4. Line two bun tins with 14 paper cases. To make the topping, put the flour, sugar and spices in a bowl. Rub in the butter until the mixture resembles fine breadcrumbs.

25 MINS TO GO

Add the bicarbonate of soda to the apple sauce and stir until dissolved. Place the butter and sugar in a large bowl and beat until light and fluffy. Lightly beat the egg and add to the mixture. Sift in the flour, cinnamon and nutmeg and fold into the mixture, adding the apple sauce a spoonful at a time.

20 MINS TO GO

Spoon the mixture into the paper cases. Scatter the topping over the cupcakes and press down gently. Bake in the preheated oven for 18–20 minutes, or until risen, golden and firm to the touch. Transfer to a wire rack and leave to cool completely.

Mini Pecan Pies

These bite-sized versions of the American classic are just right for a sweet afternoon treat or a quick dessert. They freeze well so it's worth making a double batch for another day.

Makes 12

INGREDIENTS

1 x 325-g/11½-oz sheet ready-rolled shortcrust pastry

55 g/2 oz pecan nuts

25 g/1 oz butter, plus extra for greasing

40 g/1½ oz light muscovado sugar

3 tbsp maple syrup, plus extra for glazing

1 large egg

1 tsp vanilla extract

lightly whipped cream, to serve

Variation!
For a touch of chocolate, stir 25 g/1 oz grated plain chocolate into the melted butter.

30 MINS TO GO

Preheat the oven to 220°C/425°F/Gas Mark 7 and place a baking sheet in the oven to heat up. Lightly grease a 12-hole shallow bun tin. Unroll the pastry and use a 7-cm/2¾-inch round, fluted cutter to stamp out 12 rounds. Press each round into a hole in the prepared tin.

25 MINS TO GO

Roughly chop the nuts and divide between the pastry cases. Place the butter in a saucepan over a low heat and heat until just melted. Put the sugar, maple syrup, egg and vanilla extract into a bowl and whisk with a balloon whisk until combined. Whisk in the melted butter, then carefully pour the mixture into the pastry cases, taking care not to overfill.

20 MINS TO GO

Place the tin on the baking sheet in the preheated oven and bake for 15–17 minutes, or until the pastry is golden and the filling is just set. Lightly brush the hot pies with maple syrup. Serve warm or cold with whipped cream.

Chapter **3**

FAST FAMILY CAKES & BARS

FAST FAMILY CAKES & BARS

Baking full-sized cakes and tray bakes in around 30 minutes can be quite a challenge, most take more than that time just to prepare, let alone bake. However, in this chapter you'll be amazed at what actually can be achieved in such a short time. From moist and fruity sponges to chewy granola bars and deliciously moreish chocolate brownies and blondies you'll find a whole variety of scrumptious bakes that all the family will love – there's even a hot chocolate fudge cake!

Many of these recipes are variations on classics, adapted to be baked in a fraction of the time they normally take. For example, lemon drizzle cake is usually baked in a loaf or deep round tin and needs at least 50 minutes in the oven; here we've turned it into a quick tray bake, spreading the sponge mixture in a shallow tin and baking it for half

the time. The finished result – same great zesty and moist sponge just a different shaped slice!

To make ultra-quick sponge cakes the 'all-in-one' method has to be followed but it really couldn't be easier – just place all the ingredients in a large bowl and whisk together until pale and creamy. An electric whisk is obviously an essential tool here! A little extra raising agent may be needed to give that perfect rise and if the mixture seems too firm then add a splash of milk.

To achieve perfect light and airy whisked fatless sponges every time the trick is to whisk the eggs and sugar together in a bowl set over a pan of simmering water. The heat helps to gently thicken the mixture and hold in more air. Use a very light touch when folding in the flour to

avoid knocking out any air and only bake until just springy to the touch or the sponge will have a chewy texture.

To make a chocolate Swiss roll instead of the fudge cake, roll the hot sponge up loosely with the baking paper inside and leave to cool. When cold unroll, remove the paper and spread over the fudge frosting and cream then gently roll up again.

To get the best results when baking bars and slices always use a good quality shallow cake or tray bake tin. Look for ones made of heavy gauge metal that will ensure even and quick cooking with no hot spots. To line tins quickly, cut a sheet of baking paper just a little larger than the tin and push it into the corners, snip each corner of paper at an angle and overlap the cut edges.

To store these cakes and bakes, leave to cool completely before placing in an airtight container. Most will keep for 2-3 days but the microwave cake and crispy cornflake bars are best eaten on the day of making. Brownies, blondies, chocolate polenta cake and the coconut and cherry cake will freeze well. Just pack ready-sliced into freezer bags and remove 2-3 hours before serving.

Coconut & Cherry Cake

The classic combination of sweet glacé cherries and desiccated coconut gives this ultra-quick sponge a lovely texture and fruity flavour.

Serves 10

INGREDIENTS

85 g/3 oz glacé cherries

125 g/4½ oz self-raising flour

½ tsp baking powder

2 large eggs

150 g/5½ oz butter, softened, plus extra for greasing

150 g/5½ oz caster sugar, plus extra for sprinkling

40 g/1½ oz desiccated coconut

Cook's tip!
If the glacé cherries are very sticky, place them in a sieve, rinse briefly in hot water, then pat dry with kitchen paper before chopping.

30 MINS TO GO

Preheat the oven to 200°C/400°F/Gas Mark 6. Lightly grease a 28 x 18-cm/11 x 7-inch traybake tin and line the base and two sides with baking paper. Roughly chop the cherries.

25 MINS TO GO

Sift the flour and baking powder into a large bowl. Add the eggs, butter and sugar and beat with a hand-held electric mixer for 1–2 minutes until pale and creamy. Fold in the coconut and half the cherries. Spoon the mixture into the prepared tin. Gently level the surface and scatter over the remaining cherries.

20 MINS TO GO

Bake in the preheated oven for 20–22 minutes, or until risen, golden brown and just firm to the touch. Sprinkle the top of the hot sponge with the extra caster sugar. Leave to cool in the tin for 1–2 minutes, then transfer to a wire rack to cool completely. Cut into slices to serve.

Raspberry & Almond Cake

Fresh raspberries and ground almonds give this all-in-one cake a lovely fruity flavour and moist texture. It makes a great pud served warm with cream, but is just as delicious cold with a mid-morning cuppa!

Serves 8

INGREDIENTS

115 g/4 oz self-raising flour

¼ tsp baking powder

2 eggs

115 g/4 oz butter, softened, plus extra for greasing

115 g/4 oz caster sugar

40 g/1½ oz ground almonds

175 g/6 oz raspberries

2 tbsp flaked almonds

icing sugar, for dusting

Variation!
You can vary the fruit topping – blackberries, stoned cherries or sliced pears will all work just as well.

30 MINS TO GO

Preheat the oven to 200°C/400°F/Gas Mark 6. Place a baking sheet in the oven to heat up. Grease a 23-cm/9-inch round, shallow cake tin and line the base with baking paper. Sift together the flour and baking powder into a large bowl. Add the eggs, butter and sugar and beat with a hand-held electric mixer for 1–2 minutes until pale and creamy. Fold in the ground almonds.

25 MINS TO GO

Spoon the mixture into the prepared tin. Gently level the surface and scatter over the raspberries and flaked almonds. Bake in the preheated oven for 22–25 minutes, or until risen, golden brown and just firm to the touch.

5 MINS TO GO

Leave the cake in the tin for 1–2 minutes, then turn out onto a wire rack. Serve warm or cold, dusted with icing sugar.

Blueberry Granola Bars

These delicious fruity bars are chock-full of nuts and seeds for energy on the go.

Makes 12

INGREDIENTS

50 g/1¾ oz pecan nuts

115 g/4 oz dried blueberries

225 g/8 oz rolled oats

40 g/1½ oz soft light brown sugar

25 g/1 oz sunflower seeds

1 tbsp sesame seeds

¼ tsp ground cinnamon

115 g/4 oz butter, plus extra for greasing

115 g/4 oz golden syrup

30 MINS TO GO

Preheat the oven to 180°C/350°F/ Gas Mark 4. Grease an 18 x 28-cm/ 7 x 11-inch baking tin. Chop the pecan nuts. Put the blueberries, oats, sugar, nuts, sunflower seeds, sesame seeds and cinnamon into a large bowl.

25 MINS TO GO

Heat the butter and golden syrup in a small saucepan over a low heat until just melted. Add to the dry ingredients, stirring to coat thoroughly. Transfer the mixture to the prepared tin, smooth the surface and bake in the preheated oven for 18–20 minutes, or until golden.

5 MINS TO GO

Remove from the oven and leave to cool for 1–2 minutes, then use a knife to mark into 12 bars. Leave to cool in the tin, then cut through the markings to create 12 bars.

Easy!
Simple to make, children will love helping and the bars make a great addition to school lunch boxes.

Shortcake Meringue Slices

A crisp buttery shortbread base topped with jam and a soft mallowy meringue – this is speedy baking at its best! Use any flavour jam or replace it with fresh fruit.

Makes 9 squares

INGREDIENTS

shortbread base

115 g/4 oz butter, softened, plus extra for greasing

55 g/2 oz caster sugar

175 g/6 oz plain flour

meringue & topping

2 large egg whites

115 g/4 oz caster sugar

4 tbsp strawberry jam

2 tbsp flaked almonds

Cook's tip!
If you don't have a food processor, simply place all the ingredients for the base in a bowl and mix well with a wooden spoon.

30 MINS TO GO

Preheat the oven to 200°C/400°F/Gas Mark 6. Grease a 23-cm/9-inch square, loose-based fluted flan tin. Put the butter, sugar and flour into the bowl of a food processor. Process for about 30 seconds until the mixture begins to clump together. Tip into the prepared tin and press it into an even layer in the base.

25 MINS TO GO

Bake in the preheated oven for 15–17 minutes, or until pale golden. Meanwhile, to make the meringue, put the egg whites into a clean, grease-free bowl and whisk with a hand-held electric mixer until they hold firm peaks. Gradually whisk in the sugar, a spoonful at a time, to make a firm and glossy meringue.

5 MINS TO GO

Remove the tin from the oven and spread the jam over the hot shortbread base. Spoon and swirl the meringue over the jam to cover completely. Scatter over the flaked almonds and return to the oven for 4–5 minutes, or until the meringue is pale golden. Serve warm or cold, cut into squares.

Hot Chocolate Fudge Layer Cake

With a super-speedy whisked sponge, a tub of ready-made fudge frosting and some whipped cream you really can create a rich and indulgent chocolate gateau in 30 minutes!

Serves 8

INGREDIENTS

butter for greasing

3 eggs

**85 g/3 oz caster sugar,
plus extra for dusting**

85 g/3 oz plain flour

**2 tbsp cocoa powder, plus extra
for dusting**

**225 g/8 oz ready-made chocolate
fudge frosting**

200 ml/7 fl oz double cream

**plain and white chocolate flakes
or curls, to decorate**

Cook's tip!
The whisked mixture should be thick enough to leave a ribbon-like trail on the surface when the beaters are lifted.

30 MINS TO GO

Preheat the oven to 200°C/400°F/Gas Mark 6. Lightly grease a 23-cm x 33-cm/9 x 13-inch Swiss roll tin and line the base and sides with baking paper. Put the eggs and sugar into a large bowl set over a saucepan of gently simmering water. Whisk with a hand-held electric mixer for 3–4 minutes, or until the mixture is very thick and pale (see Cook's tip!).

25 MINS TO GO

Sift in the flour and cocoa powder and gently fold in. Pour into the prepared tin and level the surface. Bake in the preheated oven for 8–10 minutes, or until risen and springy to the touch. Meanwhile, dust a sheet of baking paper with caster sugar and whip the cream until it holds firm peaks.

15 MINS TO GO

Remove the cake from the oven and immediately turn out onto the prepared baking paper. Cut the cake into 3 strips and transfer to a wire rack to cool for 5–8 minutes. Spread the frosting over the top of each strip and sandwich the strips together with the cream. Decorate with the chocolate flakes and a dusting of cocoa powder.

Apricot Flapjacks

Flapjacks are really easy to make and are great for packed lunches or fibre-packed snacks. This version is flavoured with apricots, honey and sesame seeds.

Makes 10

INGREDIENTS

175 g/6 oz margarine, plus extra for greasing

85 g/3 oz demerara sugar

55 g/2 oz clear honey

140 g/5 oz dried apricots

2 tsp sesame seeds

225 g/8 oz rolled oats

30 MINS TO GO

Preheat the oven to 180°C/350°F/Gas Mark 4. Grease a 26 x 17-cm/10½ x 6½-inch shallow baking tin. Put the margarine, sugar and honey into a small saucepan over a low heat and heat until the ingredients have melted together – do not boil. Chop the apricots. Stir the apricots, sesame seeds and oats into the melted mixture.

25 MINS TO GO

Spoon the mixture into the prepared tin and smooth the surface with the back of a spoon. Bake in the preheated oven for 18–20 minutes, or until golden brown.

5 MINS TO GO

Remove from the oven, cut into 10 bars and leave to cool before removing from the tin.

Cook's tip!
Flapjacks are still soft when they come out of the oven – they set on cooling, so don't try to remove from the tin too soon.

Blondies

For a morning coffee treat, these soft, squidgy blondies are hard to beat. Mixed in one bowl and baked in under 25 minutes they are the perfect speedy bake!

Makes 9

INGREDIENTS

115 g/4 oz butter, plus extra for greasing

225 g/8 oz light muscovado sugar

2 eggs

1 tsp vanilla extract

150 g/5½ oz plain flour

pinch of salt

85 g/3 oz white chocolate chunks or chips

Time cheat!
To save time, use a microwave-proof mixing bowl and melt the butter on high for 20–30 seconds.

30 MINS TO GO

Preheat the oven to 200°C/400°F/Gas Mark 6. Lightly grease a 20-cm/8-inch shallow square cake tin and line the base and sides with baking paper. Put the butter into a small saucepan and melt over a low heat. Transfer to a large bowl with the sugar, then beat with a balloon whisk.

25 MINS TO GO

Beat in the eggs and vanilla extract, then sift in the flour and salt and beat well until smooth. Pour the mixture into the prepared tin and level the surface with a spatula. Scatter over the chocolate chunks.

20 MINS TO GO

Bake in the preheated oven for 20–22 minutes, or until golden brown and just set (the centre will still be a little soft). Leave to cool in the tin, then remove and cut into 9 squares.

Trail Mix Bars

These soft, chewy bars with apricots and sesame seeds have peanut butter for extra flavour. Ideal for an energy boost on the go.

Makes 16

INGREDIENTS

175 g/6 oz margarine, plus extra for greasing

3 tbsp clear honey

175 g/6 oz soft light brown sugar

125 g/4½ oz smooth peanut butter

35 g/1¼ oz dried apricots

275 g/9¾ oz rolled oats

2 tbsp vegetable oil

2 tbsp sesame seeds

30 MINS TO GO

Preheat the oven to 180°C/350°F/Gas Mark 4. Grease a 23-cm/9-inch square baking tin and line with baking paper. Melt the margarine, honey and sugar in a saucepan over a low heat. Add the peanut butter and stir until everything is well combined. Chop the apricots.

25 MINS TO GO

Add the oats, apricots, oil and sesame seeds and mix well. Press the mixture into the prepared tin and bake in the preheated oven for 18–20 minutes, or until golden brown.

5 MINS TO GO

Remove from the oven and leave to cool in the tin, then cut into 16 squares.

Microwave Sponge Cake

Baking a cake in a microwave oven takes a matter of minutes, so it's perfect for a spur-of-the-moment treat. As the wattage can vary, use the cooking time as a guide or follow the manufacturer's instructions.

Serves 6

INGREDIENTS

175 g/6 oz self-raising flour

175 g/6 oz butter, softened, plus extra for greasing

175 g/6 oz golden caster sugar

3 eggs

½ tsp vanilla extract

150 ml/5 fl oz double cream, whipped

3 tbsp raspberry jam

icing sugar, for dusting

Cook's tip!
Cakes baked in the microwave dry out quite quickly so they are best eaten on the day of making.

30 MINS TO GO

Lightly grease a 20-cm/8-inch round silicone cake tin. Line a wire rack with baking paper. Sift the flour into a bowl and add the butter, sugar, eggs and vanilla extract. Beat with a hand-held electric mixer for 1–2 minutes until pale and creamy.

25 MINS TO GO

Spoon the mixture into the prepared tin and level the surface. Place in the microwave oven and cook on High for 5–6 minutes. Check the cake after about 4 minutes and every 30 seconds after that. The cake is ready when it is risen and just springy to the touch – it may still have a thin layer of wet sponge mixture on the top but this should dry out as the cake cools.

15 MINS TO GO

Leave the cake to stand for 10 minutes, then invert onto the prepared rack and leave to cool completely. Cut the sponge in half horizontally and sandwich back together with the cream and jam. Thickly dust the top with icing sugar and serve immediately.

Chocolate Brownies

These little brownies have the familiar sugary crust and soft gooey centre that we've come to know and love. They're impossible to resist, so it's a good thing they're only bite-sized!

Makes 25

INGREDIENTS

115 g/4 oz lightly salted butter, plus extra for greasing

100 g/3½ oz plain chocolate

2 eggs

175 g/6 oz light muscovado sugar

2 tsp vanilla extract

55 g/2 oz plain flour

25 g/ 1 oz cocoa powder

40 g/1½ oz pecan nuts or walnuts

Cook's tip!
It's always better to under-cook brownies as they lose their gooeyness when they are over-baked.

30 MINS TO GO

Preheat the oven to 200°C/400°F/Gas Mark 6. Grease an 18-cm/7-inch, shallow, loose-based square cake tin and line with baking paper. Chop the butter and chocolate into pieces and melt in a heatproof bowl set over a saucepan of barely simmering water. Leave to cool slightly.

25 MINS TO GO

Put the eggs, sugar and vanilla extract into a bowl and beat until beginning to turn frothy. Stir in the chocolate mixture. Sift together the flour and cocoa powder into the bowl. Chop the nuts roughly and add to the mixture. Gently stir together, then transfer the mixture to the tin and level the surface.

20 MINS TO GO

Bake in the preheated oven for 18–20 minutes, or until the crust feels dry but gives a little when pressed. Leave to cool in the tin for 1–2 minutes, then transfer to a wire rack to cool completely. Cut into 25 squares.

Chewy Marshmallow Bars

These crispy toffee and marshmallow bars will make a great treat for children — but adults will love them too!

Makes 10

INGREDIENTS

85 g/3 oz dairy toffee

55 g/2 oz butter

2 tbsp golden syrup

140 g/5 oz mini pink and white marshmallows

115 g/4 oz crispy rice cereal

2 tbsp candy-coated chocolates

30 MINS TO GO

Line a 28 x 18-cm/11 x 7-inch shallow cake tin with baking paper. Put the toffee, butter, golden syrup and 115 g/4 oz of the marshmallows into a large, heatproof bowl set over a saucepan of simmering water. Heat until melted, stirring occasionally.

20 MINS TO GO

Remove the bowl from the heat. Stir in the rice cereal until thoroughly combined. Quickly spoon the mixture into the prepared tin and smooth the surface.

10 MINS TO GO

Scatter over the remaining marshmallows and the chocolates, gently pressing them down. Chill in the refrigerator until firm. Use a sharp knife to cut into 10 bars.

Variation !
For a chocolate version, replace the dairy toffee with 115 g/4 oz milk chocolate or white chocolate, broken into pieces.

Lemon Drizzle Squares

These luscious sponge squares have a wonderful sharp yet sugary crisp topping. Made in minutes using the all-in-one technique, this is sure to become a family favourite.

Makes 9

INGREDIENTS

115 g/4 oz butter, softened, plus extra for greasing

115 g/4 oz caster sugar

115 g/4 oz self-raising flour

2 eggs

finely grated rind and juice of ½ large lemon

topping

85 g/3 oz granulated sugar

finely grated rind and juice of ½ large lemon

30 MINS TO GO

Preheat the oven to 200°C/400°F/Gas Mark 6. Lightly grease a 20-cm/8-inch shallow square cake tin and line the base and sides with baking paper. Put the butter, sugar, flour, eggs, lemon rind and juice into a large bowl and beat with a hand-held electric mixer for 1–2 minutes until pale and creamy.

25 MINS TO GO

Spoon the mixture into the prepared tin and gently level the surface. Bake in the preheated oven for 20–25 minutes, or until risen, golden and just firm to the touch. Meanwhile, prepare the topping by mixing together the sugar and lemon rind and juice in a small bowl.

5 MINS TO GO

Remove the cake from the oven and pierce the top all over with a cocktail stick. Spoon the topping over the hot cake. Leave the cake to cool in the tin – the topping will become crunchy as the cake cools. Remove from the tin and cut into squares to serve.

Cook's tip!
To extract as much juice as possible from the lemon, roll it firmly on a work surface before halving and juicing.

Cheat's Birthday Cake

If you're really stuck for time, a bought sponge cake can be transformed into a stunning birthday cake with a delicious creamy white chocolate frosting and chocolate sweet decorations!

Serves 8

INGREDIENTS

85 g/3 oz white chocolate, broken into pieces

125 g/4½ oz unsalted butter, softened

½ tsp vanilla extract

250 g/9 oz icing sugar, sifted

1 ready-made 20-cm/8-inch round Madeira or vanilla sponge cake

3 tbsp strawberry jam or raspberry jam

115 g/4 oz chocolate sweets, such as giant chocolate buttons, white chocolate jazzies and sugar-coated chocolate drops

Variation!
For a rich dark chocolate frosting, replace the white chocolate with 2 tbsp cocoa powder mixed to a paste with 2 tbsp hot water.

30 MINS TO GO

Put the chocolate into a heatproof bowl set over a saucepan of gently simmering water and heat until melted. Remove from the heat, stir until smooth, then leave to cool for 10 minutes, stirring occasionally.

25 MINS TO GO

Meanwhile, put the butter and vanilla extract into a large bowl and beat with a hand-held electric mixer until pale and creamy. Gradually beat in the icing sugar, then add the cooled chocolate and beat until smooth.

15 MINS TO GO

Cut the cake in half horizontally and sandwich back together with the jam and some of the white chocolate frosting. Place the cake on a flat serving plate. Use a palette knife to spread the remaining frosting over the top and sides of the cake. Press the chocolate sweets all over the cake in a random pattern.

Crispy Cornflake Bars

Children will love this simple bake. Best eaten on the day of making, but if there's any left over, warm it in a hot oven for a few minutes and serve with custard.

Makes 8

INGREDIENTS

butter, for greasing

1 x 320-g/11¼-oz sheet ready-rolled shortcrust pastry

250 g/9 oz golden syrup

175 g/6 oz cornflakes

85 g/3 oz chopped mixed nuts

1 egg, beaten

Cook's tip!
If you don't have ready-rolled pastry, just use 300-g/10½-oz ready-made pastry instead. Roll out on a lightly floured surface to a rectangle just larger than the tin.

30 MINS TO GO

Preheat the oven to 200°C/400°F/Gas Mark 6. Place a baking sheet in the oven to heat up. Lightly grease a 20 x 30-cm/8 x 12-inch loose-based flan tin. Unroll the pastry and use to line the tin. Trim the excess pastry by running a rolling pin over the top of the tin. Prick the pastry base and sides all over with a fork.

25 MINS TO GO

Bake in the preheated oven for 12–14 minutes, or until the pastry is pale golden. Meanwhile, heat the golden syrup in a large saucepan until runny. Stir in the cornflakes and nuts and mix thoroughly until all the flakes are coated in syrup. Stir in the beaten egg.

10 MINS TO GO

Spoon the mixture into the hot pastry case and level the surface by pressing down gently with the back of a wooden spoon. Return to the oven and bake for a further 7–8 minutes, or until the filling is crisp and golden. Leave to cool completely in the tin, then remove and cut into bars.

Chocolate Polenta Cake

A scoop of vanilla ice cream or tangy crème fraîche and a few fresh berries will turn this wonderfully moist and crumbly chocolate cake into a heavenly dinner party dessert.

Serves 6

INGREDIENTS

85 g/3 oz self-raising flour

25 g/1 oz cocoa powder, plus extra for dusting

55 g/2 oz quick cook polenta

115 g/4 oz butter, softened, plus extra for greasing

115 g/4 oz caster sugar

2 large eggs

ready-made chocolate sauce, to serve

30 MINS TO GO

Preheat the oven to 200°C/400°F/Gas Mark 6. Grease a 20-cm/8-inch round shallow cake tin and line the base with baking paper. Sift together the flour and cocoa powder into a large bowl and add the polenta, butter, sugar and eggs. Beat with a hand-held electric mixer for 1–2 minutes until thoroughly combined.

25 MINS TO GO

Spoon the mixture into the prepared tin and gently level the surface. Bake in the preheated oven for 15–20 minutes, or until risen and just firm to the touch.

5 MINS TO GO

Carefully turn out the cake onto a wire rack. Serve warm or cold, cut into thin slices (allow 2 slices per person), dusted with cocoa powder and drizzled with chocolate sauce.

Variation!
To make a lemon polenta cake, replace the cocoa powder with 25 g/1 oz self-raising flour and add the grated rind and juice of 1 lemon. Bake for 18–24 minutes.

Chapter 4
PRESTO PASTRIES & DESSERTS

PRESTO PASTRIES & DESSERTS

A quick-to-make dessert or pastry can be a lifesaver when you've spent hours preparing a special meal or when you just fancy a sweet finale without any hassle. In this chapter you'll find plenty of inspiration from crisp and flaky filo fruit tarts, warming fruit crumbles, super-quick pies as well as some really sensational show-stopping puddings including chocolate baked Alaska and banoffee meringue pie.

Fresh or frozen ready-made pastry, as well as shop bought ready-baked pastry cases are the perfect cheats when it comes to creating a fast pudding. Both can easily be bought in all the major supermarkets and taste just as good as home-made. It's always worth keeping a pack or two of ready-rolled puff or shortcrust pastry in the freezer ready to defrost and turn into a delicious dessert with a few other choice ingredients.

Remember to allow rolls of chilled pastry to stand at room temperature for a short while before unrolling otherwise the pastry may crack. Sweet and crisp ready-made pastry cases are available in various sizes and will keep for 2-3 weeks in the store cupboard.

When working with filo pastry always keep the sheets covered with a clean damp cloth or tea towel to prevent the wafer-thin pastry from drying out. The beauty of filo is any cracks can easily be patched up just by overlapping tears with a little more buttered pastry. Use a soft wide pastry brush to quickly cover the sheets with melted butter or use a scrunched piece of kitchen paper dipped into the melted butter.

Many of the recipes in this chapter are made with fresh fruit so choose whatever is in season. If you're baking the mini

130

cheesecakes in autumn, top with lightly poached blackberries and apples instead of the summer berries. To serve for a festive Christmas dessert, place a thin slice of clementine or satsuma and a sprinkling of pomegranate seeds on the top of each cheesecake or serve with a spoonful of rum-soaked dried fruits. Baked fruit tarts and pies can be filled with any fruit you like but, as the cooking time is quite short, be sure to choose ripe, sweet-fleshed fruit or use canned fruit in natural syrup.

Meringue toppings always look impressive and can be whipped up in an instant. Make sure the mixing bowl is completely grease-free before adding the egg whites. An electric whisk is an essential time-saving tool here and the whites should be whisked until holding stiff, dry peaks before gradually whisking in the sugar. Bake in a hot oven for just a few minutes until the top of the meringue turns golden brown – keep a close eye on it in the oven as the sugary meringue can quickly burn. The texture will be soft and mallowy, not crisp like a slow-baked meringue, so these desserts are best eaten on the day of making.

Cinnamon & Raisin Spirals

With a sheet of ready-rolled puff pastry and a few storecupboard ingredients, crisp, buttery home-made Danish pastries can be on the breakfast table in minutes.

Makes 12

INGREDIENTS

1 x 325-g/11½-oz sheet ready-rolled puff pastry

25 g/1 oz butter, softened

2 tbsp caster sugar

1 tsp ground cinnamon

55 g/2 oz raisins

2 tbsp apricot jam

30 MINS TO GO

Preheat the oven to 220°C/425°F/Gas Mark 7. Dampen 2 baking sheets with a sprinkling of cold water. Unroll the pastry and spread with the butter, leaving a 1-cm/½-inch border. Mix together the sugar and cinnamon and sprinkle evenly over the butter, then scatter over the raisins.

25 MINS TO GO

Gently roll up the pastry from one long side. Using a sharp knife, cut through the roll to make 12 even-sized rounds. Place the rounds, flat-side down, on the prepared baking sheets. Use the palm of your hand to flatten out each round slightly. Bake in the preheated oven for 12–15 minutes, or until risen and golden.

5 MINS TO GO

Transfer the pastries to a wire rack. Put the jam into a small saucepan and heat over a low heat until warm, then strain through a fine sieve into a small bowl to make a smooth glaze. Quickly brush the glaze over the hot pastries. Serve warm or cold.

Cook's tip!
Take the pastry out of the refrigerator about 10 minutes before you start making the pastries. This will allow it to soften slightly, making it easier to unroll.

Apple Turnovers

Quick and easy to make, these sweet pastries are a great way to use up a glut of apples.

Makes 8

INGREDIENTS

450 g/1 lb cooking apples

grated rind of 1 lemon

pinch of ground cloves

4 tbsp sugar

grated rind of 1 orange

250 g/9 oz ready-made puff pastry, thawed, if frozen

flour, for dusting

milk, for glazing

orange cream

250 ml/9 fl oz double cream

grated rind of 1 orange

juice of ½ orange

icing sugar, to taste

30 MINS TO GO

Preheat the oven to 220°C/425°F/Gas Mark 7. Peel, core and chop the apples. Mix together the apples, lemon rind and cloves. Mix together 3 tablespoons of the sugar and the orange rind. Roll out the pastry on a floured work surface into a 60 x 30-cm/24 x 12-inch rectangle. Cut in half lengthways, then across four times to make eight 15-cm/6-inch squares.

25 MINS TO GO

Mix the remaining sugar into the apple filling. Lightly brush each square with milk and place a little of the apple filling in the centre. Fold over one corner diagonally to meet the opposite one and press the edges together very firmly. Place on a baking sheet. Brush with milk and sprinkle with the orange sugar.

20 MINS TO GO

Bake in the preheated oven for 15–20 minutes, or until brown. Leave to cool on a wire rack. Meanwhile, to make the orange cream, whip together the cream, orange rind and orange juice until thick. Add icing sugar to taste and whip again until just holding soft peaks. Serve the turnovers warm with orange cream.

Time cheat! To save time, you could use ready-baked pastry cases.

Summer Berry Tarts

These little tartlets are delicious with afternoon tea or as a dessert, served with cream or ice cream.

Makes 6

INGREDIENTS

375 g/13 oz ready-rolled sweet shortcrust pastry

250 g/9 oz mascarpone cheese

1 tsp vanilla extract

1 tbsp clear honey

400 g/14 oz mixed summer berries, such as strawberries, raspberries, redcurrants and blueberries

icing sugar, for dusting

30 MINS TO GO

Preheat the oven to 200°C/400°F/Gas Mark 6. Cut the pastry into 6 squares. Place each pastry square in a 10-cm/4-inch loose-based fluted tartlet tin and ease lightly into the tin, without stretching. Trim the excess and press the pastry into the fluted sides with your fingers.

25 MINS TO GO

Place the tins on a baking sheet and prick the pastry bases with a fork. Line with baking paper and add baking beans. Bake in the preheated oven for 10 minutes, remove the paper and beans and bake for a further 5 minutes. Leave to cool for 1–2 minutes, then carefully remove from the tins and transfer to a wire rack to cool.

5 MINS TO GO

Mix the mascarpone cheese with the vanilla extract and honey, then spoon into the tartlets and spread evenly. Halve the strawberries and mix with the remaining berries, then divide between the tartlets. Dust with sifted icing sugar just before serving.

Filo Plum & Almond Tart

This crisp filo pastry with its rich almond filling is perfect for serving at the end of a special meal. You can vary the fruit – try raspberries, blueberries or thinly sliced pears.

Serves 4

INGREDIENTS

55 g/2 oz butter, softened

4 x 28-cm/11-inch square filo pastry sheets

5 small red plums

1 egg

55 g/2 oz ground almonds

40 g/1½ oz caster sugar, plus 1 tbsp extra for sprinkling

1 tbsp plain flour

custard or cream, to serve (optional)

Cook's tip!
Filo pastry can be quite fragile to handle. If cracks appear when lining the tin just brush with more melted butter and patch up any holes with a little more buttered pastry.

30 MINS TO GO

Preheat the oven to 200°C/400°F/Gas Mark 6 and place a baking sheet in the oven to heat up. Melt 15 g/½ oz of the butter in a small saucepan and use some to lightly grease a 20-cm/8-inch round, loose-based tart tin. Brush the filo pastry sheets with the remaining melted butter and layer them in the prepared tin, gently scrunching the pastry around the edge of the tin.

25 MINS TO GO

Scrunch some foil into a disc and place in the pastry case. Bake in the preheated oven for 4–5 minutes, or until the pastry is just beginning to brown around the edges. Meanwhile, quarter and stone the plums. Put the remaining butter into a bowl with the egg, ground almonds, sugar and flour and beat together until smooth.

20 MINS TO GO

Remove the foil and spread the almond mixture in the pastry case. Top with the plum quarters and sprinkle with sugar. Return to the oven and bake for 15–20 minutes, or until the pastry is golden brown and the filling is almost set (it will still be wobbly in the middle). Leave to cool in the tin. Serve warm or cold with custard, if using.

One-roll Peach Melba Pie

This simple one-roll open fruit pie is made in a fraction of the time it would take to make a normal double crust pie. It's best eaten warm from the oven with plenty of custard or cream – just take your pick!

Serves 4

INGREDIENTS

225 g/8 oz ready-made puff pastry

plain flour, for dusting

25 g/1 oz ground almonds

410 g/14½ oz canned sliced peaches in natural juice, drained

115 g/4 oz raspberries

1 egg, beaten

2 tbsp demerara sugar

cream or custard, to serve

Cook's tip!
The ground almonds help to prevent the fruit juices seeping into the pastry. You can use any other ground nuts or just a sprinkling of breadcrumbs instead.

30 MINS TO GO

Preheat the oven to 220°C/425°F/Gas Mark 7. Dampen a baking sheet with a little cold water. Roll out the pastry on a lightly floured work surface to a 23-cm/9-inch round. Place on the baking sheet.

25 MINS TO GO

Scatter the ground almonds over the pastry round, leaving a 4-cm/1½-inch border. Pile the peach slices and raspberries on top of the almonds. Brush the border with some of the beaten egg, then fold it in over the fruit, leaving most of the fruit uncovered. Brush the folded-in pastry edge with beaten egg and sprinkle over the sugar.

20 MINS TO GO

Bake in the preheated oven for 18–20 minutes, or until the pastry is crisp and golden. Serve warm with cream or custard.

Strawberries & Cream Filo Tarts

Filo pastry cooks to a golden crisp in a matter of minutes. These delectable pastry cases have a creamy custard filling topped with juicy strawberries – a perfect summer pud!

Makes 4

INGREDIENTS

25 g/1 oz butter

85 g/3 oz filo pastry

200 g/7 oz strawberries

2 tbsp strawberry conserve

150 ml/5 fl oz double cream

150 g carton ready-made custard

Get ahead!
Serve within 1 hour of filling otherwise the pastry will be soggy. You can bake the pastry a few hours in advance and fill just before serving.

30 MINS TO GO

Preheat the oven to 200°C/400°F/Gas Mark 6. Melt the butter in a small saucepan and use some of it to lightly grease four 10-cm/4-inch tartlet tins. Place the tins on a baking sheet. Use scissors to cut the pastry into sixteen 15-cm/6-inch squares.

25 MINS TO GO

Stack four squares of pastry on top of each other, each at a slight angle. Brush the top and underside of the stack with the melted butter. Press into one of the prepared tins. Repeat with the remaining pastry and butter to make four cases in total. Bake in the preheated oven for 4–5 minutes, or until golden at the edges. Carefully remove from the tins and gently flip over onto the baking sheet. Bake for a further 2–3 minutes, or until golden all over.

15 MINS TO GO

Transfer the pastry cases to a wire rack and leave to cool for 12–14 minutes. Meanwhile, hull the strawberries and slice into a bowl. Stir in the conserve. Whip the cream in a bowl until it holds firm peaks, then fold in the custard. Divide the cream mixture between the pastry cases and top with the strawberries.

Banoffee Meringue Pie

This is the ultimate cheat's dessert! Keep a ready-made pastry case and a can of dulce de leche in the storecupboard and you'll be able to impress guests at a moment's notice.

Serves 8

INGREDIENTS

1 x 20-cm/8-inch ready-made all butter round pastry case

400 g /14 oz canned dulce de leche (caramel sauce)

1 large banana

3 large egg whites

175 g/6 oz caster sugar

1 tbsp chocolate shavings

30 MINS TO GO

Preheat the oven to 190°C/375°F/Gas Mark 5. Place the pastry case on a baking sheet. Spoon the dulce de leche into the case and level the surface with a spatula. Peel and thinly slice the banana and arrange the slices on top of the caramel.

25 MINS TO GO

Put the egg whites into a clean, grease-free bowl and beat with a hand-held electric whisk until they hold stiff peaks. Gradually whisk in the sugar, one spoonful at a time, to make a firm and glossy meringue. Spoon the meringue over the bananas and swirl with the back of the spoon.

15 MINS TO GO

Bake in the preheated oven for 12–15 minutes, or until the meringue is golden brown. Sprinkle the chocolate shavings over the hot meringue and serve immediately or leave to cool. This dessert is best eaten on the day of making.

Variation!
To make individual pies, use 8 ready-made tartlet cases or press rounds of sponge into 8 small tartlet tins. Fill, then top with meringue and bake for 10 minutes.

Blueberry Tarts

Crisp, dainty pies with a moist blueberry filling and a buttery crumble top. Serve while still warm, with vanilla ice cream.

Makes 24

INGREDIENTS

300 g/10½ oz blueberries

2 tsp cornflour

55 g/2 oz caster sugar

4 tsp water

55 g/2 oz plain flour, plus extra for dusting

grated rind of 1 lemon

40 g/1½ oz butter, plus extra for greasing

325 g/11½ oz ready-rolled sweet shortcrust pastry, chilled

30 MINS TO GO

Preheat the oven to 190°C/375°F/Gas Mark 5. Lightly grease two 12-hole mini muffin tins. Put half the blueberries into a small saucepan with the cornflour, half the sugar and the water. Cook, uncovered, over a medium heat, stirring constantly, for 2–3 minutes until the juices run and the sauce thickens. Remove from the heat and add the remaining blueberries.

25 MINS TO GO

Put the flour, lemon rind, butter and remaining sugar into a mixing bowl. Cut the butter into pieces and rub in until it resembles fine breadcrumbs. Roll out the pastry on a lightly floured surface. Using a fluted cutter, stamp out 24 pastry rounds, 6 cm/2½ inches in diameter. Press into the prepared tins. Spoon the blueberry filling into the cases, then sprinkle with the topping mixture.

20 MINS TO GO

Bake in the preheated oven for 15 minutes, or until the topping is pale golden. Leave to cool in the tins for 5 minutes, then loosen with a round-bladed knife and transfer to a wire rack. Serve warm or cold.

Flapjack Fruit Crumbles

With a can of fruit pie filling and some ready-made flapjacks you can serve up this warming winter pudding in a flash!

Makes 4

INGREDIENTS

410 g/14½ oz canned summer fruits pie filling

175 g/6 oz ready-made flapjacks

55 g/2 oz flaked almonds

15 g/½ oz butter

2 tsp golden syrup

custard or crème fraîche, to serve

30 MINS TO GO

Preheat the oven to 200°C/400°F/Gas Mark 6. Divide the pie filling between four individual ovenproof dishes or ramekins. Place on a baking sheet.

25 MINS TO GO

Crumble the flapjacks into a bowl and stir in the flaked almonds. Spoon the mixture over the top of the pie filling. Dot with the butter and drizzle over the golden syrup.

20 MINS TO GO

Bake in the preheated oven for 12–15 minutes, or until the topping is crisp and golden and the filling is piping hot. Leave to cool for 5 minutes, then serve with custard.

Freezing!
You can make up double the crumble mixture and freeze half for another day. Use within 1 month, baked from frozen.

Apricot & Chocolate Meringues

Quick and easy to make, these pretty puddings look lovely served on a plate or platter.

Makes 12

INGREDIENTS

6 apricots

juice of ½ small orange

40 g/1½ oz plain chocolate

1 egg white

2 tbsp caster sugar

Variation!
When apricots are out of season, try making these with halved plums.

30 MINS TO GO

Preheat the oven to 180°C/350°F/Gas Mark 4. Halve and stone the apricots and arrange them, cut-side up, on a baking tray. Drizzle the orange juice over the top. Bake in the preheated oven for 5–8 minutes. Cut the chocolate into 12 pieces and set aside.

20 MINS TO GO

Meanwhile, whisk the egg white in a large, clean mixing bowl until it holds stiff, moist-looking peaks. Gradually whisk in the sugar, 1 teaspoon at a time, then whisk for a further 1–2 minutes, until the meringue is thick and glossy. Spoon the meringue into a piping bag fitted with a medium star nozzle.

10 MINS TO GO

Remove the apricots from the oven, but leave the oven on. Put a piece of chocolate in the centre of each apricot. Pipe a whirl of meringue on top of the chocolate. Bake for 5 more minutes, or until the meringue is tinged golden brown and just cooked. Leave to cool for a few minutes, then transfer to a serving plate.

Pumpkin Pies

These perfectly proportioned spiced pumpkin pies are ready in no time when prepared with ready-made pastry cases! Delicious warm or cold, they make a great dessert for an autumn dinner party.

Makes 12

INGREDIENTS

12 ready-made all-butter tartlet cases

200 g/7 oz canned pumpkin purée or unsweetened pie filling

70 g/2½ oz light muscovado sugar

1 egg plus 1 egg yolk, lightly beaten

2 tbsp maple syrup

125 ml/4 fl oz evaporated milk

1 tsp ground cinnamon

½ tsp ground ginger

¼ tsp ground cloves

softly whipped cream and grated nutmeg, to serve

Cook's tip!
If canned pumpkin is unavailable, steam chunks of fresh pumpkin until tender. Leave to cool, then mash with a fork until smooth.

30 MINS TO GO

Preheat the oven to 190°C/375°F/Gas Mark 5. Place the tartlet cases on a large baking sheet. Put the pumpkin purée and sugar into a large bowl and beat together with a wooden spoon.

25 MINS TO GO

Add the egg, maple syrup, evaporated milk and spices and, using a balloon whisk, mix until thoroughly combined. Carefully pour the mixture into the tartlet cases.

20 MINS TO GO

Bake in the preheated oven for 18–20 minutes, or until the filling is just set but still slightly wobbly in the centre. Serve warm or cold, topped with a dollop of whipped cream and sprinkled with a little grated nutmeg.

Easy!
A warming pudding in no time at all.

Makes 4

INGREDIENTS

2 large Bramley apples

3 tbsp maple syrup

juice of ½ lemon

½ tsp ground allspice

55 g/2 oz unsalted butter

100 g/3½ oz rolled oats

40 g/1½ oz light muscovado sugar

Mini Apple Crumbles

Everyone's favourite dessert, these delicious crumbles are delightfully individual.

30 MINS TO GO

Preheat the oven to 220°C/425°F/Gas Mark 7. Place a baking sheet in the oven to heat. Peel, core and chop the apples. Put the apples into a saucepan and stir in the maple syrup, lemon juice and allspice.

20 MINS TO GO

Bring to the boil over a high heat, then reduce the heat to medium, cover the pan and cook for 5 minutes, or until almost tender. Meanwhile, melt the butter in a separate saucepan, then remove from the heat and stir in the oats and sugar.

15 MINS TO GO

Divide the apples between four 200-ml/7-fl oz ovenproof dishes. Sprinkle over the oat mixture. Place on the baking sheet in the preheated oven and bake for 10 minutes, until lightly browned and bubbling. Serve warm.

Mini Cheesecakes with Summer Berries

These delightful individual creamy cheesecakes are perfect for a summer buffet as they can be made in advance. If you are serving a crowd, just double the quantities.

Makes 10

INGREDIENTS

40 g/1½ oz butter

85 g/3 oz digestive biscuits

250 g/9 oz full-fat soft cheese, at room temperature

85 g/3 oz caster sugar

2 large eggs

5 tbsp soured cream

2 tsp finely grated lemon rind

1 tbsp cornflour

fruit topping

115 g/4 oz small strawberries

2 tbsp strawberry jam

85 g/3 oz raspberries

55 g/2 oz blueberries

Variation!
Add 1 tbsp grated plain chocolate to the biscuit base and 25 g/1 oz plain chocolate chips to the filling. Serve with chocolate sauce instead of fruit.

30 MINS TO GO

Preheat the oven to 180°C/350°F/Gas Mark 4. Line a 12-hole muffin tray with 10 paper muffin cases. Put the butter into a small saucepan and melt over a low heat. Crush the biscuits and mix with the butter in a bowl. Divide the mixture between the paper cases, pressing it level with the end of a rolling pin.

25 MINS TO GO

Put the cheese and sugar into a food processor and process for a few seconds until smooth and creamy. Add the eggs, soured cream, lemon rind and cornflour and process for a further few seconds. Divide the mixture between the muffin cases. Bake in the preheated oven for 15–20 minutes, or until just set but still slightly wobbly in the centre.

15 MINS TO GO

Meanwhile, make the fruit topping. Hull and quarter the strawberries. Push the jam through a fine sieve to make a purée, then stir in the berries. Serve the warm cheesecakes topped with the berries or leave in the tin to cool completely, then remove and chill for 1 hour (or overnight) before serving with the berries.

Gooey Chocolate Puddings

Everyone will love these divine puddings with their hidden centres of molten chocolate.

Makes 4

INGREDIENTS

100 g/3½ oz plain chocolate

100 g/3½ oz butter, plus extra for greasing

2 large eggs

1 tsp vanilla extract

100 g/3½ oz golden caster sugar, plus extra for sprinkling

2 tbsp plain flour

icing sugar, for dusting

pouring cream, to serve

Get ahead!
To save time, prepare the puddings 1–2 hours in advance, then bake just before serving.

30 MINS TO GO

Preheat the oven to 200°C/400°F/Gas Mark 6. Grease four 175-ml/6-fl oz ramekin dishes and sprinkle with caster sugar. Break the chocolate into pieces and melt with the butter in a heatproof bowl set over a saucepan of barely simmering water. Stir until smooth. Set aside.

25 MINS TO GO

Place the eggs, vanilla extract, caster sugar and flour in a bowl and beat together. Stir in the melted chocolate mixture. Pour into the prepared ramekins and place on a baking sheet. Bake in the preheated oven for 12–15 minutes, or until the puddings are well risen and set on the outside but still molten inside.

5 MINS TO GO

Leave to stand for 1 minute, then turn out onto serving plates. Dust with icing sugar and serve immediately with cream.

Chocolate Baked Alaska

This classic meringue and ice cream combo is a real showstopper! Use a good quality ice cream that won't melt too quickly and serve as soon as it comes out of the oven.

Serves 6

INGREDIENTS

500 g/1 lb 2 oz luxury chocolate ice cream

6 ready-made chocolate brownies

2 large egg whites

115 g/4 oz caster sugar

cocoa powder, for dusting

30 MINS TO GO

Line a 700-ml/1¼-pint pudding basin with clingfilm. Place the ice cream in the basin. Slice off any excess ice cream above the rim of the basin and cut this into smaller chunks. Push the chunks into the gaps around the main block of ice cream. Top with the chocolate brownies, cutting to fit, if necessary, and press down firmly. Place in the freezer for 15 minutes.

25 MINS TO GO

Preheat the oven to 220°C/425°F/Gas Mark 7. Put the egg whites into a clean, grease-free bowl and whisk with a hand-held electric mixer until they hold firm peaks. Gradually whisk in the sugar, 1 spoonful at a time, to make a firm and glossy meringue.

10 MINS TO GO

Remove the basin from the freezer and turn out onto a baking sheet. Quickly spoon and spread the meringue all over the ice cream and the edge of the chocolate brownie base to cover completely. Bake in the preheated oven for 5 minutes, or until the meringue is just set and lightly browned. Serve immediately, lightly dusted with cocoa powder.

Variation!
For individual versions, simply top each brownie with a scoop of the ice cream, then smother in the meringue. Reduce the cooking time to 3–4 minutes.

USEFUL INFORMATION

Although many of the recipes here can be prepared with only the simplest – and most ubiquitous – kitchen utensils, there are a few items that can help you transform your kitchen from streamlined to lightning fast.

Pastry boards

These are not always necessary if you have good work surfaces. However, it was traditional to have a piece of marble on which to roll out pastry because of its cool qualities and its smooth surface, which allows the pastry to be moved around easily. If you are going to make pastry on a regular basis, it would be a sound investment to buy a specific board.

Rolling pins

In order to roll pastry well you need a heavy, smooth rolling pin. In emergencies a bottle can be used, but it does not give an even rolling. Make sure the pin is of adequate length and has a smooth finish. Pins can be bought in a variety of materials: wood is traditional but you can also buy metal and glass, which are cooler.

Pastry brushes

These brushes are useful for all sorts of jobs in the kitchen, such as brushing excess flour from pastry and for glazing with egg or milk. They are also used for greasing tins. They are available in all shapes and sizes and in various materials. Wood is traditional but plastic brushes are now available – make sure you wash and dry them well or the bristles will start to fall out.

Baking beans

For years dried beans or rice have been used to weigh down greaseproof paper or baking foil. This technique is known as 'baking blind', and enables you to cook pastry without a filling until it is crisp; the filling is added later. Today you can buy ceramic and aluminium 'beans', which have a good weight and will last forever, unlike rice and beans.

Baking trays and sheets

A good, heavyweight baking tray or sheet is a must. It is not worth buying a cheap sheet because it will buckle in the oven and possibly spill the contents. Large baking sheets should have only one upturned edge so that you can slip a large or delicate item on and off easily. Make sure the trays are not too big for the oven – leave a gap all round in order for the heat to circulate properly.

Cake tins

You need to decide what types of cake you are interested in making because there are so many shapes and sizes of tin available. Perhaps the best starting point is two 20-cm/8-inch sandwich tins, which are at least 2.5 cm/1 inch deep. They can be used for baking sponge cakes and Victoria sandwiches. Always buy the best quality you

can afford: non-stick can be helpful but they still require a light coating of oil. Make sure you wash and dry them well before storing. If you plan to bake in the microwave, you will need a silicone tin.

Bun tins

A set of 12 patty pans or a bun or muffin tray is useful for making small cakes, tarts and muffins. If you are going to bake quite frequently, or if you might make mince pies for Christmas, a second tray is helpful so that you can assemble a second batch while the first is in the oven.

Flan dishes

Tart or quiche tins are very useful for sweet and savoury dishes. Always use steel tins, because those made from porcelain or glass do not allow the food to cook properly. Loose based tins are the best because they allow you to remove the tin easily before serving; this is done by placing the flan on an upturned basin and allowing the ring to fall down. You can then transfer the flan on the base to a serving plate. A 20-cm/8-inch flan tin is the most useful size but if you have a large family or frequently cook for six or more people, a 30-cm/12-inch tin would be helpful. Small, individual tins are also available and these can be used for packed lunches or picnics.

Pie dishes

Pie dishes need to be quite deep with a good rim so that the pastry will be supported. They come in a number of sizes, usually oval or round, and can be glazed ceramic or glass. Some are made from enamel and tend to be oblong in shape. Larger ones need to be used with a pie funnel to support the pastry in the centre.

Wire rack

A wire rack allows the steam to escape from baked cakes and prevents them becoming too soggy. As soon as a cake is baked, turn it out of the tin onto an oven-gloved hand and then place it, base down, on the wire rack. This way the attractive crust on the top is maintained.

Flour sieve

Sifting flour is important, not only to ensure there are no lumps but also to introduce air. A stainless steel sieve is best, of a medium size. The sieve can also be used to strain vegetables but make sure it is always cleaned and well dried after use. Plastic versions are also available. If straining acidic ingredients, such as stewed fruit, always use a non-metallic sieve to avoid a reaction between fruit juice and metal. A very small sieve is useful for sprinkling icing sugar over cakes and desserts – you could use a tea strainer instead.

Mixing bowls

These bowls are available in stainless steel, copper, glass, plastic and glazed ceramic. A large plastic bowl with a rubber base is particularly good because the rubber base keeps the bowl steady when mixing. A metal bowl is good for whisking egg whites because it remains cool and the interior of the bowl can be kept absolutely smooth and clean. Glass, plastic and ceramic can also be used in the microwave for melting butter or chocolate.

Basins

You will need a variety of sizes for different tasks, such as beating eggs and whipping cream. A selection of small basins is ideal for assembling your prepared ingredients before starting to cook.

PREPARATION TECHNIQUES

ESSENTIAL TECHNIQUES

Baking blind

Pastry cases can be baked without a filling so that the pastry is well cooked. The tin or dish is lined with pastry and then with baking paper or foil, which is weighed down with baking beans (actual dried beans or ceramic or metal ones) to prevent the pastry bubbling up while cooking. The beans and foil are then removed and the pastry case cooked for a while longer to dry it out.

Beating

This makes food lighter by incorporating air, using a fork, a wooden spoon or an electric mixer. It is most often used for eggs, for omelettes and for cakes, beating together the butter and sugar (also known as creaming).

Crimping

This means to decorate the edges of a pie in order to ensure the edges are well sealed. This is done by pinching the pastry with a finger and thumb of one hand and pressing with the first finger of the other hand, giving a fluted edge. Crimping is also used purely decoratively on shortbread or plate pies.

Crushing

This technique is used for making biscuit crumbs for cheesecakes or flan cases. To make biscuit crumbs, put the biscuits in a large plastic bag, close the end of the bag securely and then crush the biscuits with a rolling pin.

Folding in

The term used to describe how to incorporate flour into a cake mixture. It is a gentle movement, made using a metal spoon or a plastic spatula, cutting through the mixture in a figure-of-eight movement, enabling the flour to combine without losing the air already incorporated. The same term is used in reference to meringues.

Glazing

A glaze is a finish that is brushed on to pastry before baking. It can be prepared using milk, beaten egg, or water and sugar.

Rubbing in

This is a method of making cakes, pastry and bread, where the fat is rubbed into the flour using the tips of the fingers, lifting the flour high out of the basin so that the air will be trapped in the mixture. This makes the mixture lighter.

Sifting

This is the same as sieving but refers to dry ingredients, for example sugar and flour, to remove lumps and to add air to the mixture. Shake the sieve gently over the bowl to incorporate as much air as possible.

Whisking

This is another method used to incorporate air, but it is usually used for a lighter mixture, for example egg whites or cream. To make the task easier and more efficient, you really need an electric mixer for whisking. However, a wire whisk used in a large mixing bowl with lots of energy can perform the task adequately.

169

Substitute ingredients

If you have decided to cook a recipe and discover that you don't have a particular ingredient, all is not lost. Use this list to discover if there is a way to substitute the item with a storecupboard standby.

If you need:	Quantity	Substitute:
Baking powder	1 tsp	¼ tsp bicarbonate of soda plus 1 tsp cream of tartar
Breadcrumbs, dried	40 g/1½ oz	35 g/1¼ oz cracker crumbs
Butter	225 g/8 oz	225 g/8 oz margarine, lard or vegetable shortening/200 ml/7 fl oz vegetable oil/150 ml/5 fl oz strained bacon fat
Cornflour	1 tbsp	2½ tsp arrowroot or potato starch/5 tsp rice starch
Cream, single	225 ml/8 fl oz	3 tbsp melted butter, made up to 225 ml/8 fl oz with full-fat milk (for cooking and baking only)
Eggs	1 large	2 egg yolks plus 1 tbsp cold water
Flour, self-raising	150 g/5½ oz	150 g/5½ oz plain flour plus 1 tsp baking powder and ¼ tsp bicarbonate of soda
Honey	225 ml/8 fl oz	280 g/10 oz granulated sugar plus 6 tbsp of the liquid called for in the recipe
Lemon juice	1 tsp	½ tsp vinegar
Milk		
full-fat	225 ml/8 fl oz	225 ml/8 fl oz skimmed milk, plus 2 tbsp melted butter or margarine
buttermilk	225 ml/8 fl oz	225 ml/8 fl oz natural yogurt
Soured cream	225 ml/8 fl oz	225 ml/8 fl oz natural yogurt
Vanilla extract	1 tsp	2.5-cm/1-inch piece of vanilla pod
Yogurt	225 ml/8 fl oz	225 ml/8 fl oz buttermilk or 225 ml/8 fl oz full-fat milk plus 1 tbsp lemon juice

Equivalents

Sometimes it's difficult to know what the quantity specified in a recipe means in real terms; for example 1 medium lemon will provide 3 tablespoons of lemon juice. Use this ready reckoner to establish how much of any ingredient you will need.

Food	Size or quantity	Equivalent
Apples	450 g/1lb	fresh 3 medium
Breadcrumbs	25 g/1 oz fresh	1 slice bread 25 g/1 oz dried 1 slice toast
Lemons	1 medium	3 tbsp juice/2–3 tsp zest
Limes	1 medium	1–2 tbsp juice/1 tsp zest
Oranges	1 medium	6 tbsp/125 ml/4 fl oz juice/1½ tbsp zest

Oven temperatures

Celsius	Fahrenheit	Gas Mark	Oven Heat
110°	225°	¼	very cool
120°	250°	½	very cool
140°	275°	1	cool
150°	300°	2	cool
160°	325°	3	moderate
180°	350°	4	moderate
190°	375°	5	moderately hot
200°	400°	6	moderately hot
220°	425°	7	hot
230°	450°	8	very hot

Spoon measurements

1 TEASPOON OF LIQUID = 5 ML

1 TABLESPOON OF LIQUID = 15 ML

Other measurements

Volume		Weight		Linear	
Metric	Imperial	Metric	Imperial	Metric	Imperial
50 ml	2 fl oz	5 g	⅛ oz	2 mm	1⁄16 inch
100 ml	3½ fl oz	10 g	¼ oz	3 mm	⅛ inch
150 ml	5 fl oz	25 g	1 oz	5 mm	¼ inch
200 ml	7 fl oz	55 g	2 oz	8 mm	⅜ inch
300 ml	10 fl oz	75 g	2¾ oz	1 cm	½ inch
450 ml	16 fl oz	85 g	3 oz	2 cm	¾ inch
500 ml	18 fl oz	100 g	3½ oz	2.5 cm	1 inch
600 ml	1 pint	150 g	5½ oz	5 cm	2 inches
700 ml	1¼ pints	225 g	8 oz	7.5 cm	3 inches
850 ml	1½ pints	300 g	10½ oz	10 cm	4 inches
1 litre	1¾ pints	450 g	1 lb	20 cm	8 inches
1.5 litres	2¾ pints	500 g	1 lb 2 oz	30 cm	12 inches
2.8 litres	5 pints	1 kg	2 lb 4 oz	46 cm	18 inches
3 litres	5¼ pints	1.5 kg	3 lb 5 oz	50 cm	20 inches

Index